the

VALUE-ADDED

Employee

Edward J. Cripe

the

VALUE-ADDED

Employee

Second Edition

31 COMPETENCIES

TO MAKE YOURSELF

IRRESISTIBLE

TO ANY COMPANY

EDWARD J. CRIPE AND RICHARD S. MANSFIELD

BUTTERWORTH
HEINEMANN

Boston   Oxford   Auckland   Johannesburg   Melbourne   New Delhi

∞ Recognizing the importance of preserving what has been written, Butterworth–Heinemann prints its books on acid-free paper whenever possible.

Library of Congress Cataloging-in-Publication Data
Cripe, Edward J.
  The value-added employee: 31 skills to make yourself irresistible to any company/Edward J. Cripe, Richard S. Mansfield.—2nd ed.
    p. cm.
  Includes bibliographical references and index.
  ISBN 0-7506-7451-2 (alk. paper)
    1. Career development. 2. Vocational guidance. 3. Success in business.
  I. Mansfield, Richard, 1944- II. Title.

HF5381 .C784 2001
650.14—dc21

2001043118

British Library Cataloguing-in-Publication Data
A complete record for this title is available from the British Library

The publisher offers special discounts on bulk orders of this book.
For information, please contact:
Manager of Special Sales
Butterworth–Heinemann
225 Wildwood Avenue
Woburn, MA 01801–2041
Tel: 781-904-2500
Fax: 781-904-2620

For information on all Butterworth–Heinemann publications available, contact our World Wide Web home page at: http://www.bh.com

10 9 8 7 6 5 4 3 2 1

Printed in the United States of America

Contents

v

PART 2
Guidelines for Developing 31 Core Competencies

Acknowledgments

This book is the result of the efforts of many talented and dedicated people. For their contributions, we would like to sincerely thank the following people and organizations:

- The client organizations that have provided the opportunities to apply and further refine our competency technology.
  We particularly want to thank Dennis Bankowski, Dennis Kester, Tom O'Donoghue, Monica Rottman, Joel Steffen, and Alan Russ of the American National Can Company, Walt Hogan of the Cable and Wireless organization, Theo Killion of Lane Bryant (the Limited), and Rick Shaw and Tony Wiggins of Applied Industrial Technologies.
- Gerry Plec, Jan Josephson, Marisa Gonzalez, and other Merit consultants who have helped advance our competency technology and coaching training.
- McBer & Company (now a part of the Hay Group), from where we received much of our early education and grounding on competency technology.
- Linkage, Inc. and IQPC for giving us an opportunity to share our experiences at several of their conferences.

Introduction

ABOUT THIS BOOK

We work in unsettling times. At times, the labor market is strong, unemployment is low, and organizations are competing for talent. At other times, a soft economy, mergers, consolidations, and cost containment efforts raise the specter of layoffs for others in the workforce. One thing is clear. Job security and company loyalty have gone the way of buggy whips. In this kind of business environment, how can we take charge of our work lives and control our destiny?

One way is to make ourselves more valuable to our organization. We can improve our skills, knowledge, and attitude. In other words, we can develop our competencies. By developing our competencies, we not only make ourselves more valuable to our current employers—we also become more marketable to other organizations.

This book is a guide to help employees become more self-competent, and at the same time, more self-confident. It outlines tips for developing thirty-one competencies, along with instructions on how to identify the competencies needing development. Why these thirty-one competencies? They have been selected based on the research and practical experience of the authors who have helped many organizations construct competency job models and apply those models to performance management, training and development, and selection.

This book also provides managers and coaches with practical tools to help employees develop.

For all readers, this book is intended to be used as a handbook, a toolkit of ideas, a workbook to be written in and reviewed. It can serve as a friend guiding you in your current job and helping you prepare for other career opportunities.

THERE MUST BE A PONY!

You may know the story of the boy who so relentlessly looks on the bright side that he's thrilled to receive a gift box filled with manure. As he cheerfully points out, a box of manure means that "there must be a pony!"

But most of the rest of us find it hard to hold on to optimism while looking at boxes filled with company plans for restructuring, delayering, reorganizing, outsourcing, mergers, spinoffs, and more. It's tough to be an optimist while working longer hours at pay levels that do not keep up with living costs. Where's "the pony" in reduced career opportunities, job insecurity, and ever-increasing demands by employers?

And yet, these are exciting times. There has never been a greater need for employees at all levels to be fully competent and motivated. Global competition, rapidly changing technology, and raised customer expectations are demanding more of organizations and their people. It is clear that the successful company of the future will have a sound strategy for development of competent human resources who are committed to the goals of the company.

So it is possible to be an optimist. We *can* take actions to improve our working lives. We can fight against feelings of helplessness and lack of control. We do have influence and control.

By learning about your competencies, and by enhancing and developing them, you can take control of several extremely important parts of your work life: everyday job performance; relationships with co-workers, with bosses, and with subordinates; and preparedness for other roles and careers.

FROM PATERNALISM TO PERSONAL ACCOUNTABILITY—MANAGERS AND EMPLOYEES AS COACHES

This book is also a comprehensive, easy-to-use guide for managers and others who coach and develop employees. When it comes to the performance management and career development process, most supervisors are as uneasy as those they supervise. Having a structure for assessing an employee's strengths and needs removes some of the subjectivity from coaching discussions. More important, asking employees to self-assess their competencies, with feedback, helps reduce defensiveness and creates a constructive environment for discussion.

More organizations are putting the responsibility for career development where it should be—in the hands of the employee. But employees still need support and coaching from others in the organization. Although the coaching role is usually performed by the employee's immediate supervisor, in today's boundary-less organizations, the coaching role can also be played by mentors, team leaders, project managers, and other employees.

An extremely valuable, and often underused, resource in an organization is the experienced, long-service worker who has been a superior performer. Such workers can coach others to superior performance, particularly in areas of technical expertise. The coaching role can also be performed by retirees, many of whom welcome the opportunity to continue to play a meaningful role, even on a part-time contract basis.

POLICY MAKERS AND HUMAN RESOURCE PROFESSIONALS

CEOs, presidents, division general managers, department heads, and human resource professionals can use job competency modeling to reach these goals:

- Identify existing organizational competencies and key competencies required to meet the unit's strategic plan, and implement an action plan to close competency gaps.
- Build a foundation for organizational change and improve business performance by aligning strategic and tactical planning, performance management, selection, human resource development, and succession planning.
- Integrate human resource processes into a framework that is easily understood and viewed as fair by employees.

WHY COMPETENCIES?

If the word *competency* is not a familiar one in your organization, it probably will be soon. More and more organizations are developing job competency models. These are like job blueprints, laying out the skills, knowledge, attitudes, motives, and other characteristics of superior performance. These models have a variety of uses, one being a guide for employee development.

Why are job competency models becoming popular? Because they are usually developed by studying what superior performers actually do on a job, rather than by relying on what people think constitutes superior performance. In other words, job competency models are practical, real world, and based on fact rather than subjectivity. These models can also identify the competencies that every incumbent must possess to survive in a position—the so-called threshold competencies that lead to average performance. But the really key contribution is to identify the few competencies that differentiate superior performance from average performance. With this information, organizations can change their human resource processes to select, develop, and reward superior performers and consequently increase sales and productivity, reduce costs, and achieve the organization's strategic and tactical objectives.

For example, if an organization can pinpoint the competencies demonstrated by top sales people (the top 20 percent who produce 80 percent of the revenue), it can substantially increase sales by selecting and developing a sales force with the target competencies.

Most of us strive for superior performance. We are motivated by the desire to excel, to be recognized and rewarded. This book provides guidance to help you be the superior performer your organization is looking for, with the personal benefits that accompany that level of performance.

HOW THIS BOOK IS ORGANIZED

This book is divided into three main parts.

PART 1 describes competencies and provides information and tools to assess and develop them.

- *Chapter 1* describes the purpose and use of the book, along with background on the process for selecting the thirty-one core competencies. The chapter also includes a framework for performance management, career development, and value creation.
- *Chapter 2* is about competencies, how they are acquired or developed, and how you can motivate yourself for professional development. The chapter also describes research relevant to development planning.
- *Chapter 3* provides exercises and information to help you identify specific competencies to target for development. Career planning exercises help you think more broadly about what you want to do with your life and your career.
- *Chapter 4* takes the results from Chapter 3 and adds the involvement and support of a supervisor or coach in a development plan that includes preparation, meetings, and follow-up. It also gives tips and tools for coaches and supervisors.

PART 2 is a comprehensive guide to developing thirty-one competencies. Each is explained in a format listing behaviors, importance of the competency, methods for developing and practicing the competency, methods for obtaining feedback, suggestions for managers and coaches, sample development goals, and additional resources.

- *Chapter 5* contains suggestions for developing fifteen competencies dealing with relationships with people.
- *Chapter 6* contains suggestions for developing twelve business-related competencies.
- *Chapter 7* contains suggestions for developing four self-management competencies.

The last part is an appendix of information and tools for special applications. Included is a summary of the thirty-one competencies and behaviors, reusable worksheets of the forms contained in Part 1, information on organizational uses of competency modeling for executives and human resource professionals, a sample job competency model, a list of team member and leader competencies, and a template to help evaluate the competency requirements for an open position.

WHAT THIS BOOK IS . . . AND IS NOT

We considered calling this book a manual, handbook, and guide. But all the labels still apply. What this book is *not* is a theoretical textbook or a book for managers on the latest fad or theory. And although the competency-based approach described in this book can bring substantial improvements to an organization, this book is also not meant to fix everything that may be wrong with the performance management and appraisal system of your company.

AND FINALLY . . .

We have tried to make a user-friendly book that you will read and refer to often. Please use the ample white space for notes, and feel free to copy or pull out the extra worksheets in the appendix.

We hope to periodically revise, update, and add to the resources in Part 2. You are invited to be our partner in that effort. If you know of an excellent resource for developing a specific competency, or have other suggestions for improving this handbook, please contact us at info@meritperformance.com.

PART

1

The Road to Value Creation
and Career Success

Performance Now, Career Success Next

COMPETANCIES THAT ADD VALUE

Competencies are abilities, skills, traits, and behaviors that contribute to superior performance in a job. This book identifies thirty-one core competencies and puts them in three categories: those dealing with people (Figure 1-1), business (Figure 1-2), and self-management (Figure 1-3). "People" competencies are subdivided into two clusters: (1) Leading Others and (2) Communicating and Influencing. "Business" competencies are also subdivided: (1) Preventing and Solving Problems and (2) Achieving Results.

After identifying the core competencies, the book suggests means for developing each one. It recommends practicing on the job, interviewing and observing experts, seeking feedback, reading, taking self-study courses, and performing many other activities.

The thirty-one core competencies can serve as building blocks to create competency models for key job groups within an organization. Focus groups are one way to prepare job models for each job group, such as marketing managers, operations planning managers, and supervisors. Four or more high-performing job holders and several managers form a focus group. Together they identify

- four to eight main job responsibilities
- a set of performance outcomes or measures for each job responsibility
- a set of skills and traits needed for each job responsibility
- eight to thirteen key competencies from the core set of thirty-one
- a revised set of behaviors for each key competency, describing what people in this job group need to do to demonstrate this competency

Whenever possible, focus groups should be supplemented with behavioral interviews with superior-performing job holders.

CHANGING THE APPROACH: CAREER STREAMS VS. CAREER LADDERS

How do employees and supervisors talk about career growth? Employees and managers may still think of the career ladder—good performance at one level leads to a step up to higher compensation. But this traditional concept often no longer applies because skills and job responsibilities at one level do not guarantee movement to the next level. Some organizations are creating career streams instead. The employer establishes a set of job competencies that apply to a number of different functions, or career streams, such as operations management, human resources, engineering, and finance. The employee and supervisor talk about which competencies can be developed in the present job and which ones require outside development. Employees learn about possibilities for moving from one stream to another.

The career stream concept means that job postings identify critical competencies for available positions, allowing supervisors and employees to match new-job requirements with competencies that the employee has developed in the current position.

Employees can pursue opportunities that develop additional competencies by moving across the borders of functions and through career streams. For example, one employee may move from production to information systems, another from finance to human resources. Because the organization has a number of job levels, with a range of compensation levels within each, there is plenty of opportunity for movement. It is possible to earn a higher salary without necessarily moving up to the higher grade or classification that has traditionally raised artificial barriers.

Organizations can plan for future needs by assessing which career streams are growing and which are shrinking. Employees can also be informed about the changing needs of the company.

Career development discussions are no longer about moving to the next rung on a ladder. Instead supervisors and employees focus on preparing to enter multiple career streams that share certain critical competencies. The supervisor's role is as a provider of information and opportunities. With this support, employees can strengthen existing competencies and develop a plan to use them effectively in any career move.

CAREER DEVELOPMENT: KEY CONCEPTS

Here are four concepts central to career development.

1. **Not Just for Promotion.** Employee development is not limited to upward mobility. Becoming more knowledgeable, proficient, and professional in the performance of current responsibilities can represent career development just as much as moving to a different assignment. Also, an employee can grow into new and increasing responsibilities in a position.
2. **Personal Responsibility for Growth.** No company can develop an employee who does not wish to develop. The responsibility for career planning and personal development rests with the employee. To take that responsibility, an employee must be self-aware—able to define personal goals, to determine

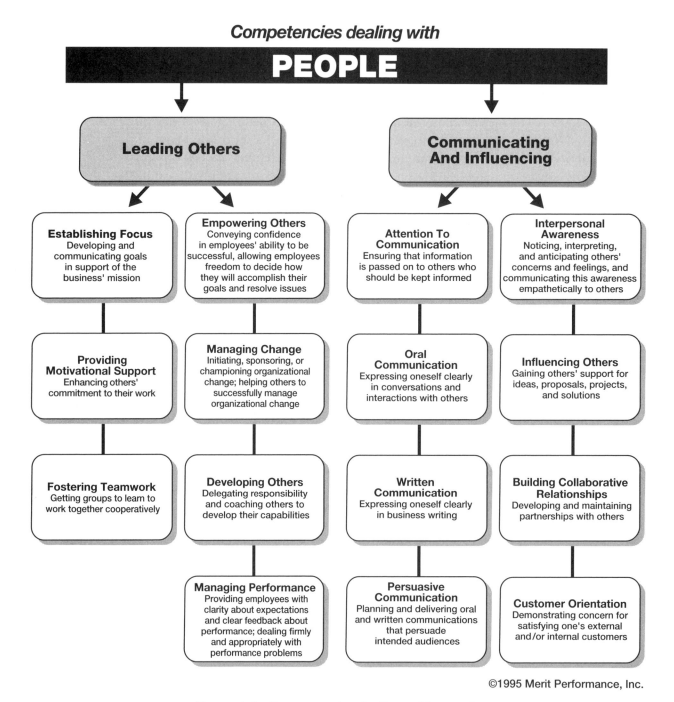

Figure 1-1. *Competencies dealing with people.*

whether these goals are attainable, to take time to evaluate prerequisite skills and knowledge, and to set priorities for starting on the chosen career path. Only the employee can answer the crucial questions, Where do I want to go? and How much am I willing to pay to get there?

3. **Interdependent Roles.** Although career development is the individual's responsibility, the organization has responsibilities too. The organization should provide the necessary coaching, counseling, structure, and more so that employees can make steady progress toward goals.

Competencies dealing with

BUSINESS

Preventing And Solving Problems

Diagnostic Information Gathering
Identifying the information needed to clarify a situation, seeking that information from appropriate sources, and using skillful questioning to draw out the information

Analytical Thinking
Approaching a problem by using a logical, systematic, sequential approach

Forward Thinking
Anticipating the implications and consequences of situations and taking appropriate action to be prepared for possible contingencies

Conceptual Thinking
Finding effective solutions by taking a holistic, abstract, or theoretical perspective

Strategic Thinking
Analyzing our competitive position by considering the market and industry trends, existing and potential customers, and strengths and weaknesses as compared to competitors

Technical Expertise
Depth of knowledge and skill in a technical area

Achieving Results

Initiative
Identifying what needs to be done and doing it before being asked or before the situation requires it

Entrepreneurial Orientation
Looking for and seizing profitable business opportunities; taking calculated risks to achieve business goals

Fostering Innovation
Developing, sponsoring, or supporting the introduction of new and improved methods, products, procedures, or technologies

Results Orientation
Focusing on the desired result of one's own or one's unit's work; setting challenging goals, focusing effort on the goals, and meeting or exceeding them

Thoroughness
Ensuring that one's own and others' work and information are complete and accurate; careful preparation for meetings and presentations; following up with others to ensure that agreements and commitments have been fulfilled

Decisiveness
Making difficult decisions in a timely manner

©1995 Merit Performance, Inc.

Figure 1-2. *Competencies dealing with business.*

4. **Honesty.** The organization and the employee must be honest with themselves. The employee must realistically assess abilities, skills, knowledge, and potential, as well as personal commitment to the chosen career path. At the same time, the company must honestly tell the employee whether career

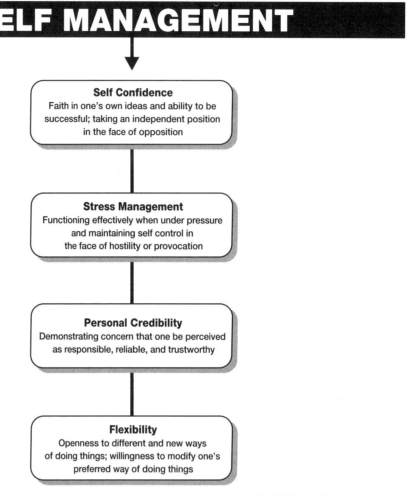

©1995 Merit Performance, Inc.

Figure 1-3. *Competencies dealing with self-management.*

objectives are feasible or probable. The manager needs to make it clear that the company cannot make promises to the employee. All the company can guarantee is that it will do its best to provide resources to facilitate employee growth that supports the attainment of corporate objectives.

THE BIG PICTURE: PERFORMANCE IMPROVEMENT AND MANAGEMENT

It is probably safe to assume that almost all of us want to improve our performance and the competencies that help us perform. So why is it so difficult for individuals within an organization and for organizations as a whole to achieve high levels of performance? Because there are many factors that influence performance. Those who are working on planning and developing competencies may find that it is also helpful to understand some key concepts about performance improvement and management.

"Systems thinking" is a way to analyze and solve human and organizational performance problems. The model shows each of us as a human performance system: We receive inputs and then use our competencies to generate outputs (Figure 1-4).

In a business setting, the inputs we receive come from our customers, internal or external. We also need clear direction about what is required, access to resources, and minimal interference. As performers, we need to have the necessary competencies, including attitude and motivation. Our output must have appropriate consequences. For doing it right, we should receive a reward, something positive such as a pat on the back. If we do it wrong, there should be negative consequences. The criteria for evaluating performance must be consistent and sound. The same benchmarks must apply to each performer. And each performer must be given feedback in the same way.

The same system applies to the performance of a team or an entire organization (Figure 1-5). The performer role is now taken by the group. Issues such as group processes, strategy, information flow, and work processes must be managed for the group to produce output effectively.

Models like these are used by organizational development consultants and performance technologists, who analyze human and organizational performance problems and create plans to improve performance. The discipline of performance management focuses on specific organizational and human resource processes such as goal setting, performance appraisal, and pay for performance. Career planning, succession planning, and progress reviews are often included in

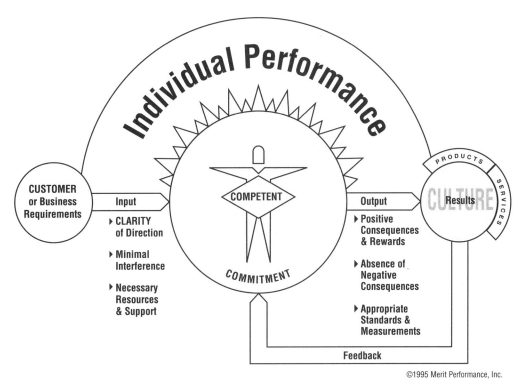

©1995 Merit Performance, Inc.

Figure 1-4. *"Systems thinking" model for an individual.*

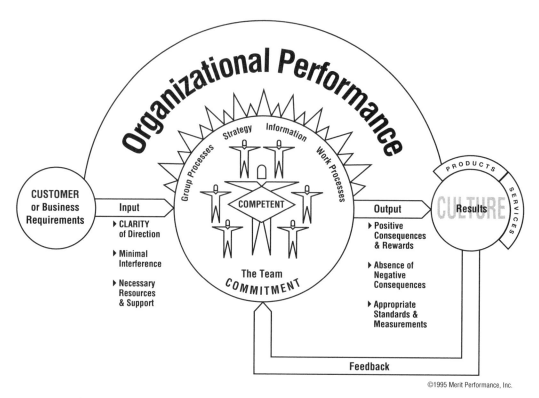

©1995 Merit Performance, Inc.

Figure 1-5. *"Systems thinking" model for a team or organization.*

performance management. The performance models show the importance of providing clear direction, selecting and developing competent employees, and providing appropriate consequences and frequent feedback.

You can see that competent performers are at the center of both performance models. Developing your own competencies or those of others is a central requirement of performance improvement. However, as the models show, competencies are only part of the entire human performance system. That means that developing additional competencies will not guarantee an improvement in performance. There are other factors that you must consider, especially if you have management responsibilities. Pay attention to all of the factors shown in the performance models, so that your organization's environment is one in which people are using their competencies well.

Development Planning and the Performance Management Process

Effective performance management can integrate professional development planning with the planning of individual business and job goals. An approach that some organizations have found effective begins with a planning meeting of an employee and manager. At that initial meeting, the employee and manager agree on a set of business and job goals—specific things the employee will do while carrying out the main job responsibilities. The employee and manager also agree on three competencies to target for professional development over the coming year. At least two of these competencies must be drawn from the set identified for the employee's job group. One competency is drawn from any others of the core set of thirty-one. This "wild card" provision enables people to address specific improvement needs and to prepare themselves for career development beyond the present job.

Using This Book to Prepare Competency Development Goals

Take these steps to prepare your competency development goals:

1. Read Chapter 2 to learn about the general process of competency development and to think about the types of activities you may want to include in your goals.
2. Read and complete the workbook pages in Chapter 3 (or in Appendix B), "How to Select Specific Competencies for Development." You will select three competencies to target for development and choose the one you will work on first.
3. Read the sections on your target competencies in Part 2, "Specific Suggestions for Developing 31 Core Competencies," to identify relevant ideas for developing them.
4. Use the workbook pages in the section "Developing Competency Goals" of Chapter 3 (or in Appendix B) to prepare a set of goals for developing each of your targeted competencies.

ADDING VALUE THROUGH EVA® & VAE®

Economic Value Added (EVA®)

Economic Value Added, or EVA, is a financial measure popularized by consulting firm Stern Stewart & Company that is intended to reflect the true economic profit of an enterprise. It is a performance measure directly linked to the creation of shareholder wealth over time.

EVA is net operating profit minus an appropriate charge for the opportunity cost of all capital invested in an enterprise. As such, EVA is an estimate of true "economic" profit or the amount by which earnings exceed or fall short of the required minimum rate of return investors could get by investing in other securities of comparable risk.

EVA = Net Operating Profit After Taxes – (Capital x The Cost of Capital)

There are three basic ways to increase value:

1. Increase the returns from the assets already in the business by running operations more efficiently without investing new capital,
2. Invest additional capital to build the business so long as expected returns on new investments exceed the cost of capital, and
3. Harvest capital from existing operations that earns insufficient returns, including selling assets that are worth more to others.

EVA can be understood via the Four M's of EVA

Measurement Adjustments are made to conventional earnings in order to eliminate accounting anomalies and bring them closer to true economic results. For example, R&D expenditures which are usually expensed, are capitalized and amortized for EVA measurement. Adjustments made are generally substantial, promote value-enhancing behavior, and are easy to communicate to non-financial managers, so that decisions are affected in a positive, cost-effective way.

Management System EVA is used as a financial management system that encompasses all the policies, procedures, methods and measures that guide strategy and operations. The goal of increasing EVA is intended to guide all managerial and operating decisions.

Motivation Incentive compensation plans are based entirely on improvements in EVA, thus motivating managers to think and act like owners. Managers earn more money by creating greater value for shareholders. Bonuses have no upside limits and are not tied to surpassing an annual budget. Therefore, budgets are driven by aggressive strategy to increase shareholder value.

Mindset An EVA system provides a common language for employees across all corporate functions. It can be a focal point for all reporting, planning and decision making and thus effect a firm's culture. It is a system of internal corporate governance that facilitates decentralized decision making and guides all employees to work in the best interests of the owners.

The Value-Added Employee (VAE®)

Value-Added Employee is a concept that expands on the importance of the human contribution to EVA. *Related principles and concepts are described throughout this book.*

There have been many efforts in recent years to measure the economic contribution of an organization's human resources. These measures have included formulas to measure the return on investment (ROI) of "intellectual capital" and "intangible assets." Particularly noteworthy are the efforts of Karl Erik Sveiby of Sweden and the Saratoga Institute in the United States.

We contend that VAE, when viewed as "value added *per* employee" will provide the best measurement of the human contribution to EVA.

VAE = EVA divided by FTEs (Full Time equivalent Employees)

The Saratoga Institute titles this metric "Human Economic Value Added." The objective of VAE or Human Economic Value Added is to shift the idea toward the contribution made by the human capital of the organization. By dividing EVA by people, we begin to think in combined human and financial terms. This is helpful for human resource professionals in that it keeps the focus on financial returns. It also keeps every executive focused on the human side, reminding them that people create value.

There are three basic ways to increase the value of an organization's human capital:

1. Increase the percentage of superior performers in the workforce through competency-based training and performance management.

2. Recruit, select and retain a higher percentage of superior performers (vs. average performers).

3. Lose or improve poor performers.

Appendix F describes a Competency Technology approach to meeting these three challenges.

A Value-Added Employee (VAE) is characterized by four fundamental qualities (the Four C's of VAE). *Also depicted in Figures 1–4 and 1–5.* These qualities are nurtured by a high performing culture (a fifth C), one that will attract, develop and retain superior performing human assets who "add value"—and support an EVA mindset.

Customer-Focus Employees are unlikely to add value without a strong focus on identifying, meeting and exceeding the requirements of both external and internal customers. Long term Net Operating Profit After Tax depends on meeting customer needs. EVA should not be construed as an "in-focused" activity, with emphasis solely on cost reduction and operating efficiency. Long term, profitable growth is what drives shareholder value. The VAE never loses sight of the main reason an organization exists, to satisfy the shareholders through profitably satisfying the customers.

Clarity The VAE must be crystal clear about his/her purpose, goals, direction, and role in the "big picture." Individual goals must be aligned with departmental and organizational goals. Most organizations assume that clarity exists—and most organizations are wrong. EVA, and the Four M's of EVA, ensure that every employee is focusing his/her attention on the critical variables that improve true economic profit.

Competence Some people perform their jobs more effectively than others. These people possess "competencies" not possessed by average performers. Employees add value when they have been hired with the right competencies and have the opportunity to develop and apply those competencies on the job.

Commitment The Motivation component of EVA's Four M's provides financial consequences that, in turn, influence commitment. But there is more. Commitment also flows from within a person (also know as "intrinsic motivation"). The VAE is committed to a higher purpose, to a core set of personal values and to a personal "mission." New ways to add value to the organization and to one's quality of life outside of work are continually pursued.

EVA® is a registered trademark of Stern Stewart & Co.

VAE® is a registered trademark of Merit Performance Group, Inc.

Capitalizing on Strengths and Building Competencies

WHAT ARE COMPETENCIES?

Competencies are the skills and personal characteristics that contribute to superior performance. Competencies include more than the technical skills needed to carry out the job tasks. For example, consider the job of the wait staff at a restaurant. Certain technical skills need to be mastered, such as carrying trays loaded with dishes, moving efficiently between kitchen and dining room, and using a calculator or computer to compute the bill. But to be outstanding, an individual must also demonstrate other qualities, such as friendliness and responsiveness to diners' concerns. Competencies for a job include both technical skills and personal qualities. Competencies are the skills and behaviors that outstanding performers demonstrate more often and with better results than do average performers.

Competencies include observable behaviors. They also include behaviors, thought processes, skills, and traits that are not directly observable. The range of competency components is illustrated in the onion-like model in Figure 2-1.

HOW COMPETENCIES ARE ACQUIRED

In most cases, competencies are probably not acquired through specific training. Instead, the person is thrust into a situation where it is important to succeed and where success depends on certain skills and behaviors. In this kind of situation, the person may try to imitate available role models, and may also try out various new behaviors. If the behaviors are successful, they become habits or skills.

In this natural acquisition process, not everyone succeeds. For those who do, success comes from a combination of situational pressure, willingness to try new behaviors, and specific aptitudes.

In addition to this natural acquisition process, there is another process by which we can develop competencies as part of a professional development program. This process has seven steps (Figure 2-2): (1) identification of the required competencies, (2) self-assessment, (3) observation and study, (4) practice, (5) feedback, (6) goal setting, and (7) support and reinforcement.

Identification and understanding of required competencies means that either through a job competency model or another means, you are able to understand

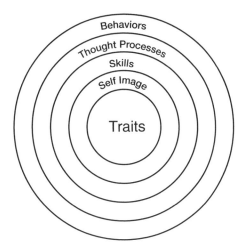

Figure 2-1. *Competency components.*

each competency well enough to recognize it in others' behavior. Studying the behavioral indicators listed under each competency (see Part 2) will help you accomplish this step. You must also be able to apply the competency to yourself, to know when you have demonstrated the competency, and when you had the opportunity to apply the competency but did not do so. To develop your understanding of a competency, think about how you can use the competency and its behaviors in your work. In which specific situations did you use the competency, and in which situations did you miss an opportunity to use it?

Self assessment means generating an accurate perception of how often and how well you demonstrate the competency. This is often a difficult step, because many people over-estimate their strengths. Research has shown that two-thirds of all employees see themselves in the top third in overall performance. To assess yourself accurately, you need honest feedback from others who can observe how you work. (Tips on how to do this are provided throughout the remainder of this book.)

Observation and study, accompanied by the other six steps, will help most people develop a competency. The way in which you learn, that is, your "learning style," will determine the ways you can effectively develop a competency. This can be done by studying the competency to understand it conceptually, by observing others, by systematically practicing certain aspects of it, or by simply trying to use the competency in a situation that calls for it.

Practice means trying out new behaviors and skills in a relatively "safe" environment, such as a training course or an activity outside work, where you can make mistakes and try to develop your skill. (Part 2 of this book contains suggested practice opportunities for each of the thirty-one generic competencies.)

Feedback means receiving constructive information that conveys the extent to which your "new" behavior is observed and is effective. The feedback from others that contributes to the accurate Self-Assessment step is also important to determine whether a competency is developing or strengthening. If you don't know how you are doing, you won't be able to modify your behavior to ensure that the competency is learned.

Goal setting means that you have established a specific goal and timetable to acquire a competency. The importance of goal setting is described later in this chapter.

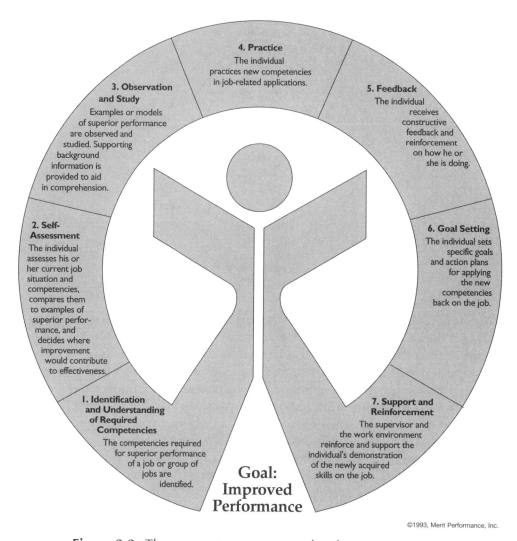

Figure 2-2. *The seven-step process to develop competencies.*

Support and reinforcement means that when you demonstrate the competency back on the job, you are made aware that "it matters." This support and reinforcement can be formal or informal, subtle or not subtle, immediate or long-term. It can be a pat on the back or satisfying appraisal discussion. It is another form of feedback and is helpful in maintaining the new behaviors of a competency.

Types of Developmental Activities

You can use a variety of developmental activities to acquire new competencies:

Readings

Readings can provide a conceptual framework for understanding a competency. This framework may be especially useful in developing the following competencies:

- Establishing focus
- Motivating others
- Fostering teamwork

- Managing change
- Managing performance
- Strategic thinking
- Influencing others

Readings can also provide ideas on how to practice or learn competencies.

Self-Study Courses

Self-study courses can provide the same advantages as readings. In addition, many self-study courses include videotapes that provide an opportunity to observe others demonstrating the competency, audio tapes making it possible to learn about the competency while driving your car, and a variety of exercises to increase your understanding and use of the competency. Self-study courses may also include tests, which allow you to check your understanding.

Seminars and Workshops

Courses provide a block of time away from the job, when you can focus on development of specific competencies or skills. Most courses provide a variety of methods (e.g., readings, videos, observation, and practice). Courses can provide opportunities to practice skills in a safe environment and to receive expert coaching. This book lists a few external courses that are offered in several geographical locations. Your organization's training staff can help you find other courses. Most programs can also be run "in-house" for an organization and tailored to the unique needs of the organization. Directories such as *The Corporate University Guide to Management Seminars,* published annually by The Corporate University Press (124 Washington Avenue, Point Richard, CA 94801), provide extensive listings of courses. The internet is also a good source of development resources. Helpful web sites include: www.seminarfinder.com, www.trainlink.com, www.trainingsupersite.com, www.tasl.com, www.trainingnet.com, www.trainet.com, and www.tcm.com/trdev/, and masterylab.com.

Observation of Outstanding Performers

Observation of outstanding performers can be useful in developing recognition and understanding of the competencies. To use this type of developmental activity, you must observe someone who is adept at the competency, and the competency must be one, such as motivating others, that is demonstrated through observable behavior.

Interviewing Outstanding Performers

Interviewing outstanding performers is easier to do than observation, because you do not have to be present with them when the competency is being demonstrated. You simply ask them to discuss how they demonstrate this competency and what they have learned about using it effectively. It is helpful to ask outstanding performers to talk about specific times when they used a competency and to talk in very specific terms about their behavior and thoughts. Interviewing outstanding performers will help you develop your understanding of the competencies. When using this method, you need not be limited to people in your own organization. Consider friends, neighbors, and people you know through professional and community organizations.

Practicing the Behaviors

Practicing the behaviors is the most direct method of competency development and is an essential part of any competency development strategy. Before practicing the behaviors, first read about or observe effective behaviors. If possible, try out the behaviors in relatively safe situations (e.g., off the job) before trying them in critical, high-stakes situations on the job.

Seeking Feedback

Seeking feedback from others provides you with an accurate self-assessment. Feedback is especially important when the competencies you are developing and refining require a high level of skill. Ask others to observe while you try to demonstrate the competency, and ask them for feedback and suggestions. Try to arrange situations where others can observe you (e.g., conducting joint sales calls or selection interviews, or managing a meeting). Let the observer know in advance what behaviors you will try to demonstrate. Ask for feedback afterward.

In preparing your plan to develop a competency, consider all of these types of activities. The more types of activities you include in your plan for developing a competency, the better your chances of success. At the same time, emphasize the activities that you are most comfortable with. Your development plan should fit your preferred style of learning.

COMPETENCY DEVELOPMENT AND YOUR PERSONAL STYLE

Think about how you would go about learning the sport of golf if you had never played before. Would you prefer to begin by reading books on the theory of a good golf swing? Or would you prefer to watch professionals demonstrate their swings? Or would you prefer to sign up for lessons and get some coaching from a pro? Maybe you would rather just get out on the course and give it a try. Each of these approaches can be helpful. To learn to play, you would probably want to use most of them, while emphasizing the types of activities that fit your own style.

If you have ever completed the Myers Briggs Type Indicator (MBTI), a widely used self-assessment personality inventory, you can use the information about your "Type" to guide your selection of developmental activities that you will be most motivated to complete.

Extroverts prefer the company of other people. If you are an *E* (**E**xtrovert), you should look for developmental activities that you can do with others, such as taking courses and talking to outstanding performers.

Introverts prefer their own company. If you are an *I* (**I**ntrovert), you may prefer developmental activities that you can do on your own, such as readings, self-study courses, and observation of outstanding performers.

Intuitives like to consider possibilities and theories. If you are an *N* (**IN**tuitive), you will probably like to read about different theories underlying the competencies you are working to develop.

Sensors like to deal with the observable aspects of a situation rather than with theories or possibilities. If you are an *S* (**Sensor**), you should look for readings or courses that set forth a step-by-step approach for using each competency. You may also prefer hands-on activities and directions for dealing with specific situations.

Thinkers rely on logic and reason to make decisions. If you are a *T* (**Thinker**), you will prefer readings and courses that provide a logical, analytical approach.

Feelers make decisions that are based on the perceived feelings of people. If you are an *F* (**Feeler**), you will prefer activities and approaches that emphasize consideration of the feelings of the people involved in situations where the competency is used.

Judgers like to plan activities and eliminate uncertainty by making decisions. If you are a *J* (**Judger**), you will probably want to have a clearly detailed development plan and to stick closely to that plan.

Perceivers value spontaneity. They do not like to plan their activities too far in advance, and they are comfortable delaying decisions. If you are a *P* (**Perceiver**), you will probably prefer a less detailed plan, which you can modify often as your situation and priorities change.

When you select developmental activities for a competency, be sure to emphasize those that fit your personal style. If the key activities are not a good match with your style, you will not be strongly motivated to complete them. Your development plan should also include some activities that do not match your personal style, even if they cause you to feel some discomfort. The more you use different ways to develop a competency, the more likely you are to achieve success.

MOTIVATING YOURSELF FOR PROFESSIONAL DEVELOPMENT

Your professional development is critical to your long-term success and to your value to your organization. Yet you may face barriers to working on your professional development. The everyday demands of your job can take all of your time and energy—if you let them. You may not get an immediate reward for taking time to work on your development plan. But if you don't take a strong interest in your development, chances are that no one else will either. If you intend to succeed, you will probably need some strategies to ensure that you have a high level of motivation.

Highlighting the discrepancy between your actual and ideal situation is a motivational technique you can use. The technique involves picturing where you would like to be several years in the future. By visualizing the size and scope of your desired job and contrasting that view with your current situation, you can consider what skills and other qualities you need to attain your goal.

Goal setting is another way to motivate yourself. Goal setting involves identifying specific, measurable action steps and committing these to writing, with dates for their accomplishment. A good goal is

- Specific
- Measurable
- Time-bound
- Realistic
- Challenging, but achievable

A good goal is *specific;* it states what action you will take with whom and when. A good goal is *measurable* so that it is clear to you and anyone else whether you have met the goal or not. Completing all the lessons in a self-study course is an example of a measurable goal. A good goal is also *time-bound;* because it has a completion date, it has a priority in relation to other responsibilities. A good goal is *realistic;* you should have at least a 50 percent chance of accomplishing it with reasonable effort. If your goals are realistic, you will begin to achieve them and to derive satisfaction from those achievements; if they are unrealistic, you will not achieve them and be less motivated to work on other goals. Finally, a good goal (or a good set of goals) is *challenging.* You should have to push yourself a bit so that you will feel true satisfaction from achieving the goal. If it is not challenging enough, you may not anticipate enough satisfaction to motivate you to work at it.

RESEARCH FINDINGS RELEVANT TO DEVELOPMENT PLANNING

Research supports the value of goal setting and has shown that specific goals lead to better performance than vaguely defined goals. And difficult goals lead to better performance than easy goals. For example, a study of performance appraisal interviews at General Electric found that improvements in performance occurred mainly when improvement needs were translated into specific goals with agreed-upon deadlines and measures of results.[1]

Other research on goal setting for personal development has shown that people who are successful in accomplishing their goals tend to be aware of forces affecting their development goals and to think about measuring their progress toward their goals.[2] Indeed, goal setting is usually effective only when people receive feedback that allows them to assess their progress toward their goals.[3]

Research also supports the importance of learning through on-the-job experience. In a study by McCall, Lombardo and Morrison,[4] successful executives reported on the experiences that had made the most difference in their professional development. Here are two key findings:

- *Learning occurs in response to organizational needs.*
  "In general, adults learn when they need to or have to, and these executives were no exception. Because of the demanding nature of these assignments, learning was not a nicety—something to be done out of interest or because it might be helpful. Learning was something these managers did because they had little choice but to take action—stab at problems even if they weren't sure what they were doing, because doing nothing was surely unacceptable. They did quick studies on unfamiliar topics, tried something, and learned from

[1] Kay, French, and Meyer. A Study of the Performance Appraisal Interview. Management Development and Employee Relations Services, General Electric New York, 1962.

[2] Kolb and Boyatzis. "Goal-Setting and Self-Directed Behavior Change." *Human Relations,* 1970, 23 (5), 439–457.

[3] Locke and Latham. "Work Motivation and Satisfaction: Light at the End of the Tunnel." *Psychological Science,* 1990, 1, 240–245.

[4] McCall, Lombardo, and Morrison. Lessons of Experience: *How Successful Executives Develop on the Job.* Lexington, MA: Lexington Books, 1988.

how it came out. They learned where they could when they could from whom they could." (p. 63)

- *Courses are effective when they address a current need.*
  "Coursework that had an impact on the executives seemed to have two things in common: it dealt with a relevant issue, and it occurred at a good time for the manager." (p. 180)

This guide applies these key research findings by

- Building the principles of goal setting into the development planning process.
- Emphasizing the importance of on-the-job learning.
- Employing on-the-job training.
- Encouraging people to construct their development plans to support their most important business needs.

Where Do You Want to Go, and What Are You Willing to Do to Get There?

CAREER PLANNING: A GUIDE TO SELF-ASSESSMENT

Before you select specific competencies to develop, spend some time thinking about your work life, personal life, and goals for the future. Your analysis should include an honest appraisal of the aspects of your job that you find satisfying and less than satisfying. Also include an assessment of your strengths and development needs. The forms on the following pages will help you with your self-assessment.

Exercise 1

The three forms that make up Figure 3-1 list the thirty-one competencies that are important in varying degrees to the functions in many jobs; each is transferable to some extent from one position to another. The competencies are in three clusters: people, business, and self-management. For some positions, a list of the most critical competencies may have already been developed in your organization. If that list is available for your position, you should refer to it. Some competencies are easier to develop on the job or through training than others. For example, improving your competency at written communication is easier than improving your self-confidence.

The first step in the self-assessment is to go through the list of competencies in Figures 3-1, 3-2, 3-3 and check the box (High-Medium-Low) that best reflects the degree to which you possess each competency. But before you check a box, consider any source of information that may be helpful, such as performance appraisals or feedback from a spouse or from people who know you well. Another technique is to write stories about previous successes that can help uncover your inherent strengths and development needs. Start with just one story—an event or time when you felt really successful. It doesn't even have to be a job-related experience; the story can come from something you achieved outside of work. It can be from any time in your life. As you write, try to include the following:

- What your goal was, what you were trying to accomplish.
- The kinds of hurdles or constraints you faced.
- What you did, step by step.
- A description of the result, the accomplishment.
- Any measurement of the result.

(text continued on page 21)

Figure 3-1. *Competencies dealing with people.*

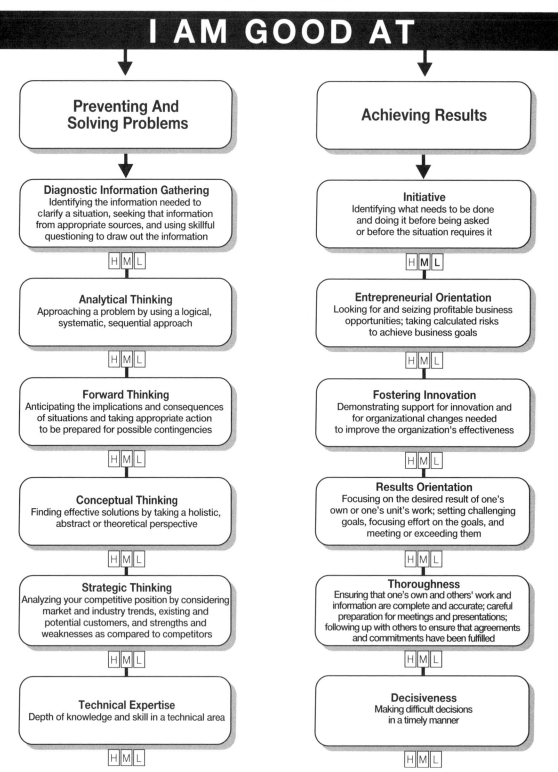

Figure 3-2. *Competencies dealing with business.*

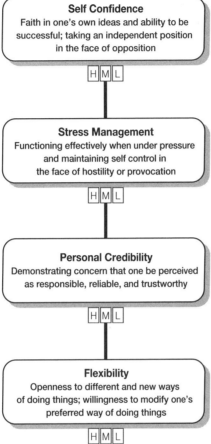

My transferable competencies dealing with

SELF MANAGEMENT

I AM GOOD AT

Self Confidence
Faith in one's own ideas and ability to be
successful; taking an independent position
in the face of opposition

H M L

Stress Management
Functioning effectively when under pressure
and maintaining self control in
the face of hostility or provocation

H M L

Personal Credibility
Demonstrating concern that one be perceived
as responsible, reliable, and trustworthy

H M L

Flexibility
Openness to different and new ways
of doing things; willingness to modify one's
preferred way of doing things

H M L

Figure 3-3. *Competencies dealing with self management.*

When you have finished the story, review it and circle any word or phrase that reveals a competency in use. Then write more stories. Include one about a time when you felt the result was unsuccessful. What does it tell you about competencies that might need development?

Exercise 2

After completing your self-assessment of the thirty-one competencies, go to the next chart, Figure 3-4, and identify your ten strongest competencies. These are the basic building blocks for success in your current job and for any future position. If you choose to change careers or compete for another position, you may

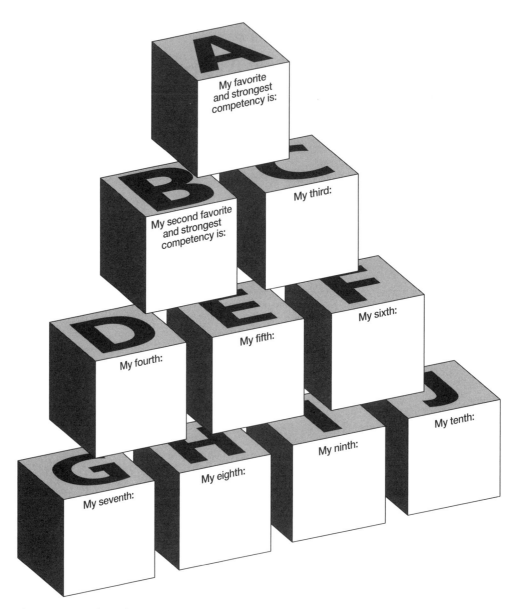

Figure 3-4. *Identifying your strongest competencies. You begin career planning and development by first identifying your transferable, functional competencies. Here you are looking for the basic building blocks of your work.*

have to rearrange your current transferable competencies into new priorities or patterns. Just as a child rearranges building blocks, you can change the arrangement of your competencies—and you may find that you have defined a new career goal for yourself.

Exercise 3

Completing the circles on the Career Planning Diagram (Figure 3-5) may lead to some additional insight about your career plans. The circle in the middle asks

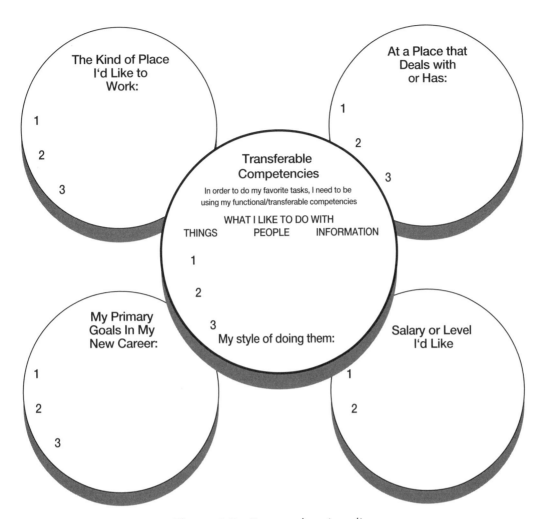

Figure 3-5. *Career planning diagram.*

you to summarize your top three transferable competencies, a continuation of the thinking you did in Exercise 2. Here are things to think about to fill out the other four circles:

- "The Kind of Place I'd Like to Work" should include your preferences about company size, number of employees, kind of business, location, department, values, organizational climate, and so on.
- "At a Place That Deals with or Has" should include the type of product or service, functional area, kind of customer, and anything else you would put to complete the sentence, "I would prefer to work for an organization that deals with or has. . . ."
- "My Primary Goals in My New Career" should include what you want to accomplish, how you want to reach your goals, the kind of team you like working on, and so on.
- "Salary or Level I'd Like" should include the salary range, starting pay level, and/or financial assistance you would need.

HOW TO SELECT SPECIFIC COMPETENCIES FOR DEVELOPMENT

This section guides you through a process for selecting three competencies to target for your professional development. You will be using the Competency Selector (Figure 3-6) and reviewing the thirty-one core competencies listed in Appendix A as well as providing responses to the questions below. Steps 1–6 below should be carried out as part of the employee's individual preparation for a development planning meeting. Step 7 is initiated at that meeting.

1. Obtain a copy of the job model or competency model for your job, if one exists. Read the job model to familiarize yourself with its contents. (An example is shown in Appendix C.)
2. If the job model or competency model specifies responsibilities or main tasks, review them. For which main responsibilities or tasks do you most need to improve your performance?
3. What are your most important job/business goals for the next six months?
4. Read the list of competencies at the end of the job model and check these off in column A of the Competency Selector. (A copy is included in Appendix B.)
5. Now use the Competency Selector and the descriptions of the thirty-one core competencies in Appendix A, together. In Appendix A, read the description of the first competency, Establishing Focus. Then, turning to the Competency Selector, decide whether to put check marks in any of columns B–F of the row for Establishing Focus. Specifically:

   • Put a check mark in column B if you believe that this competency would help you improve your performance of the responsibilities/tasks you most want to improve.
   • Put a check mark in column C, if you believe this competency would help you achieve your most important job/business goals for the next 6 months.
   • Put a check mark in column D, if this competency is needed to advance your career (i.e., if it is a competency for the next job you would like to have).
   • Put a check mark in column E, if you would rate yourself low on this competency.
   • Put a check mark in column F, if your manager or others have rated you low on this competency.

6. Repeat this process for each of the thirty-one core competencies or at least for the ones identified for your job group. This completes your individual preparation for your initial development planning meeting with your manager.
7. At the development planning meeting, review the pattern of check marks on the Competency Selector with your manager to decide on three competencies to target for development. In general, rows with four or more check marks are strong candidates. Use the last column to check three competencies.

DEVELOPING COMPETENCY GOALS

A process for developing competency goals is described below. You may begin this process at the development planning meeting with your manager, and later you should do some additional individual planning and follow-up with your manager.

For each competency you have targeted for development:

1. Read the section on this competency, in the Part 2, "Specific Suggestions for Developing Each Competency."
2. Prepare a list of six to fifteen goals you would like to include in your development plan for this competency. Each goal should specify an activity that you will complete by a specific date. Sample competency development goals are provided for each competency.
3. Draw on, but do not necessarily limit yourself to, the specific suggestions provided for developing this competency.
4. Include some goals that involve practicing the behaviors of the competency in relatively safe situations, where mistakes will not have serious consequences.
5. Include some goals that involve practicing the behaviors of the competency in situations that will help you achieve your job or business goals.
6. Create a list of goals for this competency that is both realistic and challenging. Assume that you will focus on one competency for a 3–4 month period and that you will spend 3–6 hours per week in addition to your regular job responsibilities working on your competency goals.
7. Review a draft list of the goals for this competency with your manager and get his/her input.
8. Enter the competency development goals on a copy of the Competency Development Planning Form (Figure 3-7).
9. Repeat this process for the two other competencies you have targeted for development.

Employee: _____ Date: _____

Instructions: If there are competencies identified for your job, check these competencies in column A. Read the definition and behaviors for each competency, beginning on page 40. Then check any boxes that apply in columns B–G. After completing this process for all thirty-one competencies, use column G to select three competencies to target for your personal development.

	A	B	C	D	E	F	G
	IDENTIFIED FOR MY JOB	IMPROVE PERFORMANCE OF RESPONSIBILITIES I MOST NEED TO IMPROVE	SUPPORTS MY KEY JOB GOALS FOR NEXT 6 MONTHS	NEEDED FOR CAREER ADVANCEMENT	SELF ASSESSMENT IS LOW	SUPERVISOR'S OR OTHERS' ASSESSMENT IS LOW	SELECTED TO DEVELOP
1 Establishing Focus							
2 Providing Motivational Support							
3 Fostering Teamwork							
4 Empowering Others							
5 Managing Change							
6 Developing Others							
7 Managing Performance							
8 Attention to Communication							
9 Oral Communication							
10 Written Communication							
11 Persuasive Communication							
12 Interpersonal Awareness							
13 Influencing Others							
14 Building Collaborative Relationships							
15 Customer Orientation							
16 Diagnostic Information Gathering							
17 Analytical Thinking							
18 Forward Thinking							
19 Conceptual Thinking							
20 Strategic Thinking							
21 Technical Expertise							
22 Initiative							
23 Entrepreneurial Orientation							
24 Fostering Innovation							
25 Results Orientation							
26 Thoroughness							
27 Decisiveness							
28 Self Confidence							
29 Stress Management							
30 Personal Credibility							
31 Flexibility							

Figure 3-6. *Competency selector.*

Employee: _____ Manager: _____ Date: _____

Competency Targeted for Development: _____

Reasons: _____

Specify the 3–4 month period when you will work on this competency: _____

COMPETENCY DEVELOPMENT GOALS	TARGETED COMPLETION DATE	ACTUAL COMPLETION DATE

Signatures:

Employee: _____ Manager: _____

Figure. 3-7. *Competency development planning form.*

CHAPTER 4

Obtaining the Resources and Support You Need

THREE STAGES OF GIVING AND RECEIVING HELP

Chapter 2 discussed some concepts to help you motivate yourself for professional development and presented some research findings relevant to development planning. In the last chapter, you had an opportunity to dig deeper and analyze your strengths and development needs, your likes and dislikes, and your career aspirations and then select specific competencies to target for development.

Sometimes the task of developing competencies is affected by other factors that complicate a seemingly simple activity. Most of us already know what we are good at and not so good at, and yet, we may have a hard time doing something about our weaknesses. Sometimes it takes a critical incident such as a missed deadline, a poor performance appraisal rating, or a lost promotion opportunity to get our attention. And for some of us, it takes something even more serious, such as getting fired, to motivate us to action.

Keep in mind that "action" does not always mean developing new competencies. Getting into a career or position that makes the best use of your existing competencies and is forgiving of your shortcomings may be a better option. For example, if you are an innovative, big-picture kind of person who does not like handling or analyzing details, you should make sure you have someone, such as a top-notch administrative assistant, to help you with the details of your position or you should avoid positions where success is dependent on detail orientation and analytical thinking.

In cases where the better choice is to develop or enhance our competencies, what usually takes place in order to go from an awareness of a need to concrete action? Several thought processes and actions take place on two different levels: one level is in the mind of the employee and the other is in the mind of the coach (usually the person's manager). There are three essential stages, represented in Figure 4-1, that we go through before taking action.

Stage 1: Awareness

In this stage, the employee becomes aware that a problem exists. Independently, or with the help of a coach, the employee sees a gap between actual performance and desired performance, or a gap between demonstrated competencies and required ones. This stage often occurs during a performance review or progress review meeting, but should also occur as the result of ongoing coaching discussions. The acknowledgment that an opportunity for improvement exists usually creates energy for both the employee and manager to change.

Stage 2: Acceptance

Even with awareness and energy for potential change, it is possible for the employee to not fully "own" the problem. Defensiveness, highlighted by "excuses" that other factors and people outside the employee's control are contributing to or causing the problem, is common. Recognizing nonacceptance can be difficult because it often is unspoken. Probing, asking the right questions, and listening by the coach are required.

Total acceptance requires that an employee not only acknowledge the problem, but also that he or she cares about it being a problem. For example, an employee who becomes aware of having poor interpersonal skills late in his or her career may not care enough about the problem to do anything about it.

Acceptance means that the employee is truly motivated to change; and the motivation must come from within. The manager or coach can help by being supportive and providing clear, consistent feedback and advice regarding options. Managers do not need to become amateur psychologists. Just being authentic and having the courage to honestly tell another person what may be happening, even if wrong, goes a long way in building the kind of trusting relationship that leads to improved performance and job satisfaction.

Stage 3: Planning

At this stage, the employee wants help and is ready to begin the hard work of planning actions that will lead to improvements. With the help of the manager and other coaches, such as a mentor or a human resource representative, specific goals for development are established. Attempts should be made to write goal statements with the same degree of precision given to business goals. However, it is sometimes difficult to write a competency development goal so that its achievement can be measured precisely. One option is to write action plans that include the listing of observable behaviors that indicate the demonstration of a competency.

Completing these stages does not mean that improvement will in fact take place. Ongoing feedback, support, monitoring, coaching, counseling, reviewing, and modifying goals and action plans are also needed.

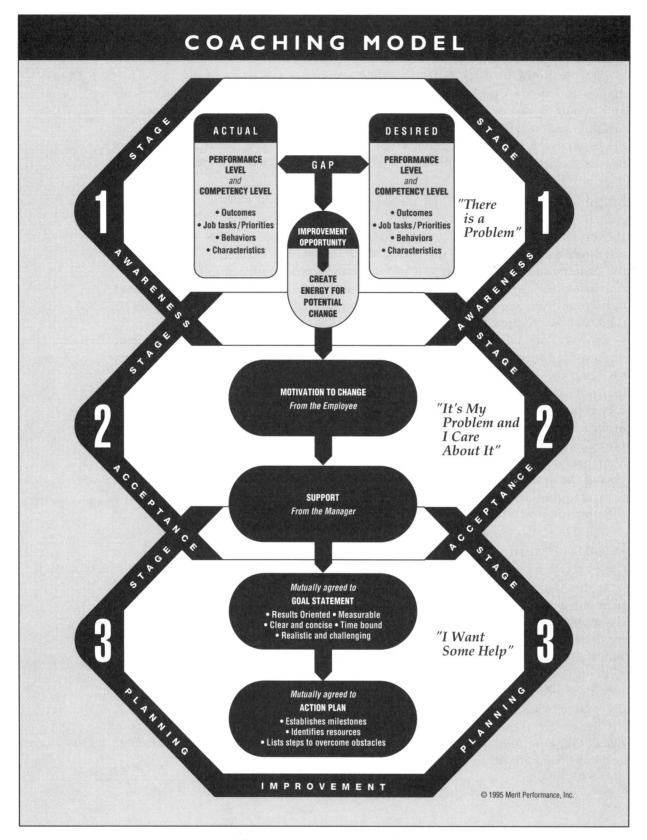

Figure 4-1. *Coaching model.*

EIGHT STEPS TO CREATING A COMPREHENSIVE DEVELOPMENT PLAN

Below is an eight-step development planning process, applicable in any organization, followed by a description of what should happen in each step. This is a continuation and elaboration of the work done in Chapter 3. Organizations or work units can modify this process to accommodate specific requirements regarding formal meetings, procedures, and required documents. The eight steps are as follows:

1. Individual Preparation
2. Initial Planning Meeting
3. Preparation of a Draft Development Plan
4. Review and Modification of the Draft Development Plan
5. Signing and Filing the Development Plan
6. Implementing the Plan
7. Periodic Progress Review Meetings
8. Preparation of New Development Plans

1. Individual Preparation

Using and consolidating the work done in Chapter 3, you should prepare for the initial development planning meeting by

- Reviewing all available information about the job description, job responsibilities, and competencies required for the job.
- Assessing his/her performance and identifying areas for improvement in the job responsibilities or specific job tasks.
- Preparing specific, measurable job goals for the next 6–12 months such as "Develop and implement ways to reduce order preparation time from 24 hours to 4 hours" or "Develop and provide safety training to unit employees."
- Thinking about the next desired job and the competencies required for this job.
- Reviewing the competencies and thinking about ones to target for development.

The employee's manager prepares by

- Reviewing all available information about the job description, job responsibilities, and competencies required for the job.
- Assessing the employee's performance and identifying areas for improvement in the job responsibilities or specific job tasks.
- Thinking about possible job goals for this employee for the next 6–12 months.
- Thinking about the next possible job for this employee and the competencies required for this job.
- Reviewing the competencies and thinking about ones for this employee to target for development.

2. Initial Planning Meeting

At an initial development planning meeting, the employee and manager should

- Discuss and, if necessary, clarify the main job responsibilities and the performance outcome measures for these responsibilities.
- Discuss how well these responsibilities are being carried out; identify areas for improvement.
- Agree on specific job or business goals for the next 6–12 months.
- If appropriate, discuss career development and the next possible job for this employee.
- Review the competencies for the job.
- Discuss which competencies are needed to improve performance and achieve the job or business goals.
- Select three competencies for the employee to target for development over next year and one competency to focus on for first 3–4 months.
- Review this book to develop ideas for developing these competencies.
- Set a date within 2 weeks to review the draft development plan to be prepared by the employee.
- Set a date to review progress in about 3 months.

3. Preparation of a Draft Development Plan

The employee drafts separate lists of three to ten goals for developing each competency. It is most effective to focus on the goals for one competency at a time. (See sample format on pages 151–152 in Appendix.)

4. Review and Modification of the Draft Development Plan

The manager reviews the draft development plan and may suggest revisions. The employee then prepares a revised development plan.

5. Signing and Filing the Development Plan

The employee and manager both sign the development plan. Each retains a copy, and a third copy may be sent to the organization's human resource department. The human resource department can review all plans and help coordinate developmental activities that cross department boundaries.

6. Implementing the Plan

The employee implements the plan by

- Setting aside 3–6 hours per week for development activities.
- Carrying out the planned activities.
- Keeping a weekly log of activities and results.
- Seeking assistance and resources from the manager and others, as needed.

7. Periodic Progress Review Meeting

The employee and manager meet at least every 3–4 months to review progress and discuss any revisions needed in the development plan.

8. Preparation of New Development Plans

Once a year the employee and manager start the process again, beginning at Step 1. The employee should target new competencies for development, if

- Previously targeted competencies have been developed.
- New job responsibilities or goals require development of additional competencies.
- The employee is preparing for a job requiring new competencies.

ROLES IN THE DEVELOPMENT PLANNING PROCESS

Your Role as an Employee Includes:

- Owning the responsibility for your development.
- Initiating the competency assessment process on a regular basis (once or twice a year).
- Initiating development planning meetings with your supervisor.
- Creating a development plan.
- Following through on your development plan.
- Seeking and accepting opportunities that will enhance your development.
- Recording in a development planning journal each week your progress, ideas, feedback, issues, and concerns related to your developmental activities.
- Being prepared to discuss progress on your development plan at the year-end review and quarterly reviews with your manager.

Your Manager's Role Includes:

- Meeting with you to review your development planning activities, as part of the year-end and quarterly review meetings.
- Providing specific, constructive feedback about how you are performing, based on his/her own observations and on feedback received from others.
- Reviewing your development plan and providing helpful suggestions.
- Providing coaching and suggestions about how you can be more effective.
- Leading the discussion of the progress you have made on your development plan at the year-end and quarterly review sessions with you and providing resources (money, equipment, people) to help you accomplish your goals.
- Helping you develop relationships with a network of people within the organization.
- Running interference for you with upper management and other groups within the organization.
- Providing encouragement, support, and reinforcement for your efforts at professional development.

The Role of Your Coworkers Includes:

- Reviewing your development plan and suggesting ways to improve it.
- Providing useful feedback and suggestions, if asked, about your attempts to use the competencies.
- Telling you how they have handled the kinds of situations and problems that arise in your job.
- Working with you to provide on-the-job coaching and training.
- Observing your behavior in public situations (e.g., presentations, sales calls) and later providing constructive feedback and suggestions.
- Providing resources and opportunities.
- Offering support when you are feeling frustrated.

FOR COACHES AND MANAGERS

While the primary purpose of this book is the self-development of competence, rather than the supervisor's or manager's role, we are including a summary of tips for supervisors and coaches that may be helpful.

As a coach or supervisor, you have a special responsibility in the development of an employee. Your observations about an employee's demonstrated competencies (or lack of demonstrated competencies) and the way in which your observations are communicated to the employee will have an enormous impact on his or her acceptance of the feedback. The following are key points that describe some ways you can effectively carry out your coaching role.

You play a dual role as employee and supervisor. It will be difficult for you to be helpful to others if you are not committed to your own self-development. Practice the competency assessment and competency building techniques in this book and write up a development plan for yourself. If necessary, practice the "influencing others" and communications competencies to gain the support of your supervisor and others.

You play a dual role as supervisor and coach. A key role of each supervisor is to coach others. As organizations downsize, rightsize, reorganize, reengineer, merge, etc., the contribution, or value added, of managers and supervisors is constantly questioned. The transfer of knowledge to others and the development of their competencies remain as primary purposes of a supervisory position.

The coaching role can be performed by others. In some organizations, the coaching role is also played by people who are not immediate supervisors. Some people are better coaches than others. They possess competencies that contribute to superior coaching (see below). This may include having technical knowledge gained through experience and/or education that needs to be transferred to others. Therefore, employees can have more than one coach. The concept of mentoring applies here. Mentors, usually senior-level people, help "junior" people develop the competencies needed for career advancement.

Competencies for Coaching and Performance Management

If you have a coaching role, or a desire to play a coaching role, you may want to look closely at specific competencies (out of the list of 31) that correlate more directly with superior coaching. When constructing your own development plan, ask yourself which of the following competencies are strengths and which are areas where improvement is needed.

- Diagnostic Information Gathering and Analytical Thinking. The accuracy of the data you gather and the observations you make about the behavior of someone you are coaching or supervising forms the foundation for productive feedback and coaching meetings. A poor use of these competencies leads to arguments, conflicts, and demotivated employees and coaches.
- Establishing Focus. This is essential to providing direction and establishing goals for business results and competency development.
- Managing Performance. This includes behaviors for providing direction, standards, and follow-up to ensure that the entire work unit achieves its goals.
- Developing and Empowering Others and Interpersonal Awareness. These are behaviors that are critical to establishing and maintaining an on-going coaching relationship that is built on trust.

The material in Part II contains detailed descriptions of ways to build these competencies and become a more effective coach and/or supervisor.

SUGGESTED PROCESS FOR THE CAREER DEVELOPMENT MEETING: HOW MANAGERS CAN MAKE IT EFFECTIVE

Preparation for the Meeting

- Accumulate as much background information about the employee as you can—his/her job experience, educational qualifications, and previous performance results.
- Ask the employee to develop his/her own career plan.
- Be ready to furnish the employee with objective data about the organizational world in which he/she is expected to function. For example, have available facts and figures about promotions, how they are made and how frequent they are. Know the personal and professional requirements of different positions, educational and development opportunities, transfer possibilities, and details of the retirement program.
- Develop an agenda for the meeting. Remember to keep it in front of you during the meeting to avoid becoming sidetracked.
- Schedule the meeting at least one week in advance. Remember to plan sufficient time, hold calls, and meet in a comfortable and private area.

Conducting the Meeting

- Greet the employee in a warm, friendly manner to help reduce some of his/her anxiety.
- Begin by reviewing the purpose and desired outcomes of the meeting. Include a summary of the agenda you have prepared; ask the employee what additions he/she would like to make.
- Clarify that the success of the session is a dual responsibility and encourage the employee to actively participate in the process.
- Get the employee's perception of his/her aspirations, interests, personal traits, and personality dynamics.
- Help the employee to assess his/her own background and qualifications.
- Encourage the employee to evaluate his/her capabilities shrewdly and relate them to the realities of the organization and his/her long-term potential in it.
- Be honest and candid in your estimate of the employee's potential.
- Encourage the employee to consider a wide range of options or alternatives.
- Help the employee develop a plan of action that will support his/her long-range career goals. Identify both on-the-job and off-the-job resources that will help the employee achieve his/her goals and that you, as manager, are willing to support.
- Summarize the discussion by reviewing all decisions made, and confirm your support and interest in the employee's future.
- Establish a means for monitoring progress and set a date for a follow-up meeting.

Follow-Up

- Have the employee write up his/her understanding of what was discussed and outline the specific plan of action on the career development form. (See Appendix B, pages 153–154.)
- Make yourself accessible to the employee for further consultation.

PART

2

Guidelines
for
Developing
31 Core
Competencies

CHAPTER
5

Competencies Dealing with People

1. ESTABLISHING FOCUS

Definition: The ability to develop and communicate goals in support of the organization's mission.

An employee demonstrating this competency:

- Acts to align own unit's goals with the strategic direction of the business.
- Ensures that people in the unit understand how their work relates to the business' mission.
- Ensures that everyone understands and identifies with the unit's mission.
- Ensures that the unit develops goals and a plan to help fulfill the business' mission.

Importance of this Competency

This is a key leadership competency because it involves providing direction and meaning to people's work. By establishing focus, you can motivate your staff, establish teamwork, and maximize the chances of achieving your most important business goals.

General Considerations in Developing this Competency

To use this competency, you must first ensure that you have a clear understanding of the strategic direction and plans for the overall organization and business. Then, with your staff, you should make a strategic analysis of your own unit. Who are its internal and external customers? What are its existing and potential strengths? What should its mission be? What does it need to do to support the strategic direction of the overall business? If you want your staff to support you, you should involve them in answering these questions. Next, you should develop a plan for the unit that includes both short-term and longer-term goals. This should be done with the involvement and participation of people in your unit. Finally, you should communicate the plan clearly and repeatedly, to ensure that everyone in the unit understands it and is setting personal goals in alignment with it.

Developing this competency involves strategic thinking, planning, facilitation, and communication skills. Because this competency is complex, it is important to develop a broad understanding of what you should do and the various means for accomplishing it. The best way to learn this competency is to work with a leader or consultant who is using it. If this is not possible, consider learning from experts: leaders who have demonstrated this competency in your own or another organization. It may also be useful to read books describing this process.

When you have an understanding of what you want to do, consider obtaining some help. Ideally, consider enlisting an internal or external consultant to work with your unit and facilitate the process. If this is not possible, seek feedback and suggestions from the most knowledgeable persons you can find, on what you plan to do, before doing it.

Practicing this Competency

Obtain and read documents about the strategic direction of your organization, business, and department.

Invite the management of the larger unit (e.g., organization, business, plant, department) to meet with your unit to discuss the larger unit's strategic direction and what your own unit can do in support of that strategic direction.

Interview your unit's internal customers or invite them to meet with the staff of your unit. Ask the internal customers to identify their goals and needs and ways your unit can support them.

Meet with the employees who report directly to you to review information about the business's strategic direction and decide what your unit should do to support that strategic direction. Consider what changes should be made. Find out with what other groups should your unit be cooperating? Whose support should you obtain? Develop a plan with specific action steps, dates for their accomplishment, and persons accountable for each step.

Share your unit's plan with your management and ask for feedback and suggestions.

Communicate your unit's plan to everyone in the unit. Consider multiple vehicles for communication. Include a meeting(s) in which people have a chance to voice their suggestions, questions, and concerns.

Keep a copy of your unit's plan available (e.g., on flip charts) and use every opportunity to explain decisions and actions by referring to the plan.

Periodically (at least quarterly) review and update the unit's plan.

Obtaining Feedback

After a unit meeting to establish focus or develop a plan, conduct an exercise to "pro/con" the meeting. On a flip chart draw a vertical line and write "Pro" and "Con" at the top of each column. First ask people what went well. Capture responses in the "Pro" column. Then ask what could have been done better. Capture responses in the "Con" column.

Before a unit meeting to establish focus or develop a plan, review your agenda and planned process with someone whose judgment you respect. Ask for suggestions. After the meeting, ask a participant for feedback about your process and facilitation.

Learning from Experts

Interview someone who has successfully established focus for a business or organizational unit. Consider people both inside and outside of your organization and company. Ask that person to walk through the process. How did he/she decide to approach the task? Why? What specifically did he/she do? What would you have seen and heard if you had been present? Obtain descriptions of what happened at key meetings. What problems or issues arose? How did the person deal with these problems or issues? What, if anything, would the person do differently.

Coaching Suggestions for Managers

If you are coaching someone who is trying to develop this competency, you can:

- Model the process in your unit so that the person you are managing can see how to go about this process.
- Arrange for the person to meet and talk with others in the organization who have established direction in their units.
- Meet with the person and the staff in his/her unit to explain the larger business goals and direction of your unit and provide your perspective on what the person's unit needs to do to align itself with the direction of the larger unit.
- Help plan communications and provide your suggestions and feedback.

Sample Development Goals

By December 1, I will interview Mary Jones and Curt Morrow to learn how they established focus in their organizational units.

By November 15, I will read *The Leadership Challenge,* by James Kouzes and Barry Posner, and prepare a written list of ideas that I can implement in establishing focus in my own unit.

By November 8, I will obtain and review the business's strategic plan and prepare a list of ideas about how my unit can specifically support the business's strategic plan.

By December 15, I will have my plant manager speak to my unit about the plant's strategic direction and what our unit should do to support the plant's strategic direction.

By February 1, I will hold a meeting with my unit to develop a plan for the unit, with specific tasks, accountabilities, and dates for their accomplishment.

By February 15, I will hold a meeting with all unit staff to present and review the unit plan.

Books

2020 Vision: Transform Your Business Today to Succeed in Tomorrow's Economy by Stan Davis and Bill Davidson. New York: Simon & Schuster, 1992.

On Becoming a Leader by Warren Bennis. Reading, MA: Addison-Wesley, 1989.

The Change Masters by Rosabeth M. Kanter. New York: Simon & Schuster, 1983.

Competitive Strategy by Michael Porter. New York: Free Press, 1980. Provides a conceptual framework for developing a business strategy—often a key aspect of a vision.

Managing Beyond the Quick Fix by Ralph Kilmann. Jossey-Bass, 1989. Provides a high-level discussion of how to implement organizational change.

The Leadership Challenge by J. M. Kouzes and Barry Z. Posner. Code E76ATA, if ordered through Pfeiffer & Co., tel.: 1-800-274-4434.

The Seven Habits of Highly Effective People by Stephen Covey. Especially Habit 2: Begin with the End in Mind. Can be ordered through Covey Leadership Center, 1-800-553-8889.

Seminars and Workshops

Managerial Skills for Experienced Managers. Three days. American Management Association Course. Various locations. Tel. 518-891-0065. Mtg. No. 2525T23.

Operational Planning. Two days. UA Consulting & Training Services. Various locations. Tel. 619-552-8901. Code: OP-PC.

Applied Strategic Planning. Three days. UA Consulting & Training Services. Various locations. 619-552-8901. Code: ASP-PC.

Managing Performance—With Competence. (Adding Value through PM.) Three days each. MasteryLab. Tel. 1-800-870-9490.

REACH™ Coaching Performance Excellence. Two days. MasteryLab. Tel. 1-800-870-9490.

Developing Value-Adding People and Adding Value (for employees). One-Two days each. MasteryLab. Tel. 1-800-870-9490.

Other Resources

The Seven Habits of Highly Effective People by Stephen Covey. Six audio cassettes. Order through Nightingale Conant, 1-800-525-9000. Code786PAS.

2. PROVIDING MOTIVATIONAL SUPPORT

Definition: The ability to enhance others' commitment to their work.

An employee demonstrating this competency:

• Recognizes and rewards people for their achievements.
• Acknowledges and thanks people for their contributions.
• Expresses pride in the group and encourages people to feel good about their accomplishments.
• Finds creative ways to make people's work rewarding.
• Signals own commitment to a process by being personally present and involved at key events.
• Identifies and promptly tackles morale problems.
• Gives talks or presentations that energize groups.

Importance of this Competency

Providing Motivational Support is a key competency distinguishing leaders from managers. It is by providing motivating support that a manager gets results through other people. The productivity and creativity of your unit is likely to depend to a significant degree on your ability to keep your staff motivated. The emphasis here is on self motivation, with the manager responsible for creating an environment in which each employee feels motivated to perform at a superior level.

General Considerations in Developing this Competency

Your own behavior and personal style contributes to your effectiveness in motivating others. If you demonstrate a high energy level and a positive attitude, even in the face of difficult situations, others are more likely to respond in the same way. Conversely, if you demonstrate low energy, frustration, anxiety, or tension, others are also likely to respond in kind.

Another aspect of this competency is to demonstrate genuine interest and responsiveness to the people you manage. If your Interpersonal Awareness is strong, you can use that competency to help motivate others. Make sure that your people have access to you, especially when they have a problem or concern. Your responsiveness to their concerns will be motivating.

A third way to use this competency is to show appreciation to others for their contributions and work. Too many managers take good work for granted and provide feedback only when a subordinate makes a mistake. A key part of motivating others is recognizing and rewarding people for their contributions.

Practicing this Competency

Make a point of noticing and praising each employee's best work.

If someone goes above and beyond normal job requirements, acknowledge this effort publicly, if possible.

Find ways to celebrate accomplishments, especially when the whole unit is involved. Holding a pizza party is one possible way to celebrate.

Try to learn what motivates each person in your unit. What is each person trying to achieve? What are his/her interests outside of work? What kind of work does he/she most enjoy? Use this knowledge in making work assignments.

If you notice a morale problem in your group, take action. First, talk with your people to understand what is causing the problem. If possible, do something about it.

Develop your public speaking skills and practice giving energizing talks.

Obtaining Feedback

Ask a coworker whom you trust to observe you over a one-month period and tell you when you are doing things that are positively motivating (acknowledging people's efforts, praising desired behavior, staging group celebrations of accomplishments, speaking in an energizing way) and when you are doing something that decreases others' motivation (e.g., losing your temper, showing signs of stress, demonstrating irritability, criticizing others in a non-constructive way).

Get the people who report directly to you together and tell them that you are working on this competency and would like their help. Tell them that you will be asking them once a week to give you feedback about specific things you did that they found positively motivating and negatively motivating. Then, on a weekly basis, get them together for a few minutes and ask these questions:

• What did I do that was positively motivating?
• What did I do that was negatively motivating?
• What else could I do that would be positively motivating?

Capture people's responses on flip-chart pages. Listen and accept people's ideas. It may be helpful to summarize and paraphrase what you have heard (e.g., "You're saying that when I criticized your report, you felt unmotivated because you had taken a lot of time to develop the recommendation"). If you express disagreement or try to defend yourself, your direct reports are likely to conclude that you really don't want honest feedback, and they will stop providing it.

Learning from Experts

Identify someone who is good at keeping people motivated. Interview this person about what he/she does to keep people motivated positively. Ask for specific examples of what the person did and how he/she did it. Ask what this person has done to build teamwork. Ask for examples of how this person gives negative feedback in a constructive way.

Try to work on a team headed by someone who is good at motivating others. Observe how this person (a) acknowledges people's contributions, (b) builds teamwork, and (c) expresses disagreement in a constructive way.

Coaching Suggestions for Managers

If you are coaching someone who is trying to develop this competency, you can:

• Model this competency by acknowledging this person's contributions and ideas and by staging celebrations of team accomplishments.

- Assign this person to work on a team headed by someone who is good at motivating others.
- Acknowledge and praise behaviors that are positively motivating.
- Provide constructive feedback and suggestions when you observe behavior that is harmful to others' motivation.
- Encourage the person to come to you to plan interactions (group meetings or one-on-one sessions) that will be positively motivating.

Sample Development Goals

Over the next two weeks, I will praise some behavior or accomplishment in each of the people who report directly to me.

By March 15, I will plan and stage a celebration for some accomplishment by my unit (e.g., hitting a key milestone in the commercialization process).

By December 20, I will meet individually with each person who reports directly to me to try to learn what each person likes and dislikes about his/her work, what each person's career goals are, and what each person's personal interests are outside of work.

By November 15, I will interview Sandy Duncan about what she does to keep her people motivated.

From now through January 20, I will observe Bill Thomas, who is team leader for the Cost Improvement Team, and take notes on what he does that is effective in motivating that team. I will identify at least five ideas that I can apply on the Communication Team.

By March 1, I will read *Performance Management* by Aubrey Daniels and make a list of ideas to apply in my unit. By April 15, I will apply at least five of these ideas in my unit.

Books

Performance Management by Aubrey Daniels. Tucker, Georgia: Performance Management Publications, 1989.

Motivating at Work: Empowering Employees to Give their Best by Twyla Dell. Order through Crisp Publications. 1-800-442-7477. ISBN 1-56052-201-1.

1001 Ways to Reward Employees by Bob Nelson, Workman Publishing, 1994.

Self-Study Courses

How to Recognize and Reward Employees. American Management Association Self-Study Course. 1-800-262-9699. Stock # 80192CYI. Includes four audio cassettes.

Seminars and Workshops

Developing Executive Leadership. Three days. American Management Association Course. Various locations. Tel. 518-891-0065. Mtg. No. 2501T23.

Motivating Others: Bringing Out the Best in Your People. Three days. American Management Association Course. Various locations. Tel. 518-891-0065. Mtg. No. 2275TX5.

3. FOSTERING TEAMWORK

Definition: As a *team member*, the ability and desire to work cooperatively with others on a team; as a *team leader*, the interest, skill, and success to get groups to work together.

Team members demonstrating this competency:

- Listen and respond constructively to other team members' ideas.
- Offer support for others' ideas and proposals.
- Are open with other team members about their concerns.
- Express disagreement constructively (e.g., by emphasizing points of agreement, suggesting alternatives that may be acceptable to the group).
- Reinforce team members for their contributions.
- Give honest and constructive feedback to other team members.
- Provide assistance to others when they need it.
- Work for solutions that all team members can support.
- Share their expertise with others.
- Seek opportunities to work on teams as a way to develop experience and knowledge.
- Provide assistance, information, or other support to others to build or maintain relationships with them.

Team leaders demonstrating this competency:

- Provide opportunities for people to learn to work together as a team.
- Enlist the active participation of everyone.
- Promote cooperation with other work units.
- Ensure that all team members are treated fairly.
- Recognize and encourage the behaviors that contribute to teamwork.

Importance of this Competency

Fostering Teamwork is a critically important competency. Increasingly in organizations, important work must be done by teams. Teamwork is becoming more important in natural work units, as organizations attempt to empower their workforces. There are fewer supervisors, and their role is changing from an emphasis on direction and control to an emphasis on facilitation of self-directed teams. In addition to natural work units, which need teamwork to function effectively, important tasks are assigned to cross-functional teams, comprised of persons with the right combination of skill sets to accomplish the task.

Everyone should be able to work constructively as a team member, and many people need to develop the skills of team leadership.

General Considerations in Developing this Competency

The best way to learn about teamwork is to work on an effective team with an effective team leader. In addition, books on teams and team leadership are also useful. If you are leading a team, it may be helpful to seek advice and coaching from others with extensive experience leading teams.

Practicing this Competency

As a team member, you can:

• Listen to others' ideas and proposals.
• Support others' ideas and proposals.
• Suggest an idea that builds on someone else's idea.
• Express disagreement constructively (e.g., "What I like about Bob's idea is. . ., and I wish there was a way to. . .").
• Be open with other team members about your concerns.
• Recognize and reinforce the contributions of other team members.
• Give honest and constructive feedback to other team members.
• Work for a solution that everyone on the team can support.
• Offer to help others on the team.
• Provide assistance when other team members ask for it.

As a team leader, you can:

• Create a team to tackle an important task.
• Enlist everyone's active participation.
• Ensure that all team members are treated fairly.
• Recognize and encourage the behaviors that lead to teamwork.
• Learn about a team problem-solving or decision-making method and bring it to the team.
• Ensure that there is a clear agenda for each team meeting.
• Facilitate the group process so that the team accomplishes its agenda.
• Ensure that the team has a plan with specific action steps that specify what will be done, by whom, and by what deadlines.
• Provide constructive feedback to team members regarding their team participation.
• Periodically ask the team to reflect on its own behavior and to identify what it is doing effectively and less effectively and what it needs to do to become more effective.

Obtaining Feedback

Ask one or two team members or the entire team to give you constructive suggestions for improving your team behavior. Possible questions include:

• What am I doing that is helpful and constructive?
• What am I doing that is less constructive?
• What could I do more of that would make me more effective as a team member?

Ask someone to observe you at a team meeting and to provide suggestions to help improve your team performance.

Learning from Experts

Join a team that is led by a skilled team leader. Observe this person and take notes on what this person does that seems effective. Notice how this person

- Prepares for team meetings.
- Keeps the meeting to its planned agenda.
- Helps the team select and implement processes for problem solving, planning, and decision making.
- Gives feedback to team members.
- Recognizes and reinforces behaviors contributing to teamwork.
- Deals with disagreement and conflict.

Interview a skilled team member. Ask this person what he/she does to lead a team effectively. Ask for specific examples.

If you are planning to try something new with a team, ask for suggestions and advice.

Coaching Suggestions for Managers

If you are coaching someone who is trying to develop this competency, you can:

- Help this person get onto a team led by a skilled team leader.
- Model effective team leader behaviors yourself.
- Sit in on a team meeting, observe the person, and provide constructive feedback afterwards.
- Make yourself available to talk to the person about what is happening on his/her team and to provide suggestions.

Sample Development Goals

For a Team Member:

At the team meeting on October 26, I will reinforce the contributions of three other team members.

At the team meetings on November 11 and 15, I will try to express disagreement in a constructive way. After the meeting, I will ask another team member for feedback about how well I did this.

At the team meeting of December 2, I will facilitate the team's development of an action plan for implementing the new accounting procedures.

I will ask Jane Louden to observe my team behavior over the next three team meetings (through December 16) and give me feedback and suggestions on my team behavior.

By January 12, I will read *The Team Handbook: How to Use Teams to Improve Quality* by P. Scholtes, identify a set of ideas to use on our Manufacturing Quality Team, and present these ideas to the team.

For a Team Leader:

At the next team meeting, set for October 10, I will ask for everyone's ideas on the commercialization proposal.

By February 4, I will read *Effective Group Problem Solving* by William Fox, and try out its group problem-solving method with the Market Analysis Team.

By October 30, I will interview Dave Wellin about the things he has done to manage teams effectively.

By March 4, I will hold a meeting with my team at which I will ask for feedback and suggestions about what I can do to be more effective as a team leader.

By May 15, I will read *50 Activities for Team Building* by G. Parker and R. Kropp, identify several team building activities to try out with the Distribution Team, and try out at least two team-building activities. Afterward, I will ask the team for feedback on each activity.

Books

The Wisdom of Teams by Jon Katzenbach and Douglas Smith. Order through Pfeiffer & Co., 1-800-274-4434, Code #H76AT1.

How to Lead Work Teams: Facilitation Skills by Fran Rees. Order through Pfeiffer & Co., 1-800-274-4434, Code # 659AT1.

How to Meet, Think, and Work to Consensus by Daniel Tagliere. Order through Pfeiffer & Co., 1-800-274-4434, Code # 995AT1.

Empowered Teams: Creating Self-Directed Work Teams that Improve Quality, Productivity, and Participation by R. Wellins, W. Byham, and J. Wilson. Order through Pfeiffer & Co., 1-800-274-4434, Code # G03AT1.

Team Building: An Exercise in Leadership by Robert Maddux. Order through Crisp Publications. 1-800-442-7477. ISBN 1-56052-118-X.

Building Productive Teams by Glenn Varney. Order through American Society for Training and Development, 1-703-683-8100. Order Code VABP.

Faultless Facilitation by Lois Hart. Order through American Society for Training and Development, 1-703-683-8100. Order Code HAFF.

The Team Handbook by Peter Scholtes. Order through Oriel, Inc., 800-669-8326.

Management Teams by Meredith Belbin, Butterworth–Heinemann, 1996, 1-800-366-2665.

Self-Study Courses

How to Build High-Performance Teams. American Management Association Self-Study Course. Tel.: 1-800-262-9699. Stock #94076CYI.

Managing and Resolving Conflict. American Management Association Self-Study Course. Tel.: 1-800-262-9699. Stock #94022CYI.

Managing Conflict. American Management Association Self-Study Course. Tel.: 1-800-262-9699. Stock #80186CYI. Includes 4 audio cassettes.

How to Plan and Run Effective Meetings. American Management Association Self-Study Course. Tel.: 1-800-262-9699. Stock #94051CYI.

Effective Team Building. American Management Association Self-Study Course. Tel. 1-800-262-9699. Stock #80090CYI. Includes six audio cassettes.

How to Lead Successful Project Teams. American Management Association Self Study Course. Tel. 1-800-262-9699. Stock #80172CYI.

Seminars and Workshops

Developing High-Performance Teams. Three days. American Management Association Course. Various locations. Tel. 518-891-0065. Mtg. No. 2523T23.

The Effective Facilitator: Maximizing Involvement and Results. American Management Association Course. Various locations. Tel. 518-891-0065. Mtg. No. 2578TX5.

Developing High Performing Work Teams. Three days. UA Consulting & Training Services. Various locations. Tel. 619-552-8901. Code: HPT-PC.

Effective Team Building. Three days. UA Consulting & Training Services. Various locations. Tel. 619-552-8901. Code: ETB-PC.

Leadership and Teamwork. Three days. Center for Creative Leadership. Tel. 336-545-2800.

Developing High Quality Performance in Teams and Task Forces. NTL Institute. Five days. Tel. 800-777-5227.

Creating and Sustaining High Performing Teams. Five days. NTL Institute. 1-800-777-5227.

TeamWorks™. Three days on-site for intact teams. TeamWorks™ for Team Leaders. Three days. MasteryLab. Tel. 1-800-870-9490.

High Performance Teaming. Two days. Institute of Entrepreneurship and Executive Education. Tel. 800-672-7223, Ext. 5092.

Other Resources

The Five-Star Team Builder. 17 minute video. Order through Talico, Tel. 904-241-1721. Code TAL-104.

4. EMPOWERING OTHERS

Definition: The ability to convey confidence in employees' ability to be successful, especially at challenging new tasks; sharing significant responsibility and authority; allowing employees freedom to decide how they will accomplish their goals and resolve issues.

An employee demonstrating this competency:

- Gives people latitude to make decisions in their own sphere of work.
- Is able to let others make decisions and take charge.
- Encourages individuals and groups to set their own goals, consistent with business goals.
- Expresses confidence in the ability of others to be successful.
- Encourages groups to resolve problems on their own; avoids prescribing a solution.

Importance of this Competency

Empowerment, the successful sharing of decision-making and problem-solving responsibilities is important to organizations for at least four reasons. *First,* it enables faster decisions and more responsiveness to internal and external customers and thus enhances an organization's productivity and competitiveness. *Second,* empowerment leads to better utilization of people's skills. Empowered employees, who perform a wider variety of tasks, develop the skills to do these tasks; and managers, who spend much less time monitoring and controlling, can focus on activities that are often neglected, such as strategic planning and staff development. *Third,* employees who are empowered develop more self-confidence and higher morale. *Finally,* many of the new organizational forms that are being developed to increase competitiveness, such as self-managed teams and flatter, less hierarchical organizations, require empowerment to be successful.

General Considerations in Developing this Competency

Developing this competency does not require much in the way of new skills; it is more a matter of rethinking your approach to management. If your management style has emphasized control—giving orders, making decisions, and monitoring performance, empowerment will require significant change on your part. Unless you build the groundwork for this change, it is likely to be unsuccessful. The danger is that you will share authority, your employees will make poor decisions, you will take back authority, and everyone will be unhappy about what happened.

To successfully empower others, you must build the groundwork for change and implement it gradually by

- Discussing and clarifying expectations about your new role as a coach and resource provider and the employees' new roles as responsible and accountable problem solvers and decision makers.
- Ensuring that employees get any training they will need.
- Ensuring that employees have access to the information they will need.

- Providing guidelines and parameters regarding limits of empowerment.
- Using leading questions to coach and model the processes of problem solving and decision making.
- Recognizing and praising behaviors reflecting responsible decision making and problem solving.
- Creating a climate where experimentation is encouraged and mistakes are treated as opportunities for learning.

You can learn more about implementing this competency by talking to someone who has done it successfully and by reading books on this topic.

Practicing this Competency

Talk to an employee or to a group of employees and explain what you would like to do in terms of empowering them. Clarify what your own role will be and what role you would like the employee(s) to have.

Coach a group through a decision-making process by asking questions that lead the group through the thinking process required to make a good decision. Use questions like these:

- What are the criteria for a good decision in this case?
- What information do I have that will be needed?
- What additional information do I need, and how can I get it?
- What are the alternatives?
- How should I go about choosing among the alternatives?
- What are the risks associated with each alternative?

Empower an individual or group to make a decision or solve a problem. Be sure you have provided the resources and information needed to do this effectively.

Over a two-week period make a point of noticing and praising behaviors that indicate that your employees are successfully demonstrating empowerment.

Obtaining Feedback

After a period in which you have empowered employees to make a certain kind of decision or solve a certain type of problem, lead a debriefing and learning session on a particular decision or problem. Find out what the employee(s) did and how, and ask the group to identify learning points—things that you or they could do differently in the future. Keep the focus on learning, not on blaming.

Periodically ask employees about their perception of how the empowerment process is going. Ask what you can do differently to make the process more effective.

Learning from Experts

Interview someone in your own or another organization who has successfully empowered employees. Ask how the person went about the process, what worked and what didn't, what problems were encountered, and how the person addressed them.

Coaching Suggestions for Managers

If you are coaching someone who is trying to develop this competency, you can:

- Model the process of empowerment with this person.
- Help the person develop a plan for empowerment.
- Discuss how the process is going and offer feedback and suggestions.
- Assign this person to a team or task force headed by someone strong in empowerment.

Sample Development Goals

By December 2, I will meet with my employees, explain empowerment, and clarify expectations about their role and mine.

By December 10, I will interview Sandy Dunbar to learn how she has empowered the staff in her unit.

By December 20, I will hold a session with my team, to coach them through the process of planning a bid.

By January 10, I will read *Empowerment in Organizations* by Vogt and Murrell and make a list of ideas that I can apply with my Production Team.

Books

Empowerment in Organizations by Judith Vogt and Kenneth L. Murrell. Order through Pfeiffer & Co., 1-800-274-4434, Code #555ATI.

Zapp! The Lightning of Empowerment by William Byham. Order through amazon.com or barnesandnoble.com.

The Leadership Challenge: How to Get Extraordinary Things Done in Organizations by J. Kouzes and B. Posner. Code No. E76ATA, if ordered from Pfeiffer & Co., tel: 1-800-274-4434.

Participative Management: Implementing Empowerment by L. Plunkett and R. Fournier. Code H15ATA, if ordered through Pfeiffer & Co., 1-800-274-4434.

The Empowered Manager by Peter Block. Jossey-Bass, 1989.

Self-Study Courses

Shared Leadership: Developing a Strategy for Success. American Management Association Self-Study Course. 1-800-262-9699. Stock #95004CYI.

Getting More Done Through Delegation. American Management Association Self-Study Course. 1-800-262-9699. Stock #92029CYI.

Seminars and Workshops

Managing Performance—With Competence. (Adding Value through PM—for Staff). Three days each. MasteryLab. Tel. 1-800-870-9490.

5. MANAGING CHANGE

Definition: The ability to demonstrate support for organizational changes needed to improve the organization's effectiveness; initiating, sponsoring, and implementing organizational change; helping others to successfully manage organizational change.

An employee demonstrating this competency:

- Personally develops a new method or approach.
- Proposes new approaches, methods, or technologies.
- Develops better, faster, or less expensive ways to do things.

A manager/leader demonstrating this competency:

- Works cooperatively with others to produce innovative solutions.
- Takes the lead in setting new business directions, partnerships, policies, or procedures.
- Seizes opportunities to influence the future direction of an organizational unit or the overall business.
- Helps employees develop a clear understanding of what they will need to do differently as a result of changes in the organization.
- Implements or supports various change management activities (e.g., communications, education, team development, coaching).
- Establishes structures and processes to plan and manage the orderly implementation of change.
- Helps individuals and groups manage the anxiety associated with significant change.
- Facilitates groups or teams through the problem-solving and creative-thinking processes leading to the development and implementation of new approaches, systems, structures, and methods.

Importance of this Competency

Managing Change means identifying what an organizational unit needs to do differently in the future and developing and implementing plans for change. This competency is important because most organizations need significant, ongoing change in structure, work processes, procedures, and styles of management. To remain competitive, organizations need many people with the drive and skill to identify and implement these changes.

Without this competency, organizations will either fail to implement changes or implement them poorly, with loss of productivity and employee morale.

General Considerations in Developing this Competency

Part of what is needed to develop this competency is a new attitude about your role: an attitude that emphasizes taking initiative, demonstrating a sense of urgency, persisting in the face of resistance, and refusing to accept the status quo.

In addition to a change in attitude, this competency also requires developing some knowledge and skill in the processes and tools of organizational change.

The best way to acquire this knowledge and skill is by participating in an organizational change process led by a skilled leader or consultant. If possible, ask an internal or external consultant to guide your team through the process of change and to teach some of the techniques and tools.

Because this is not always possible, you may have to use other methods. You may be able to take a course on change management offered by an internal or external consultant. You can learn some of the tools for change by reading some of the references in this section. You can also learn by doing: planning and implementing a change, reflecting on what has worked effectively and less effectively, and planning next steps accordingly.

This competency builds on many other competencies, such as Fostering Teamwork, Empowering Others, Establishing Focus, Providing Motivational Support, Interpersonal Awareness, Influencing Others, and Persuasive Communication. If you are also working on one of these competencies, you will learn techniques that can be applied in Fostering Innovation.

Practicing this Competency

Organize a team to identify new directions or procedures for your unit.

Volunteer to serve on a team charting change for a larger part of the organization than your unit.

Organize a meeting of the people in your unit to discuss and clarify what they will need to do differently as a result of changes in the organization.

Try out a team problem-solving or decision-making process that you have read or heard about with a team on which you are a member.

Obtaining Feedback

Each time you try out a new change management process (e.g., for planning, team decision making, team problem solving) hold a session with the team to discuss what went well and what could be done differently and better in the future.

Learning from Experts

Volunteer to serve on a cross-functional team charged with implementing change. Observe what the team leader does, and keep a list of ideas to apply in your own unit.

Interview someone who has successfully led an organizational unit through change. Consider people outside of your own organization, as well as people within it. Ask the person to walk you through the process he/she led. Find out how the person approached this situation and what he/she specifically did. Ask about problems that were encountered and how they were addressed.

Coaching Suggestions for Managers

If you are coaching someone who is trying to develop this competency, you can:

- Assign the person to work on a team headed by a consultant or internal leader who is skilled in change management.
- Help the person develop a plan for working with his/her unit to implement change. Think through the resources and support this person will need. Try

to anticipate and develop contingency plans for problems that may be encountered.

- Make yourself available on a regular basis to discuss how the change management efforts are progressing.

Sample Development Goals

By March 15, I will hold a meeting with the staff in my unit to review the overall direction of the division and identify what our unit should do differently to implement this direction and to develop a plan for change.

By April 10, I will identify a new group problem-solving method and try it out in my unit.

By May 1, I will read *Corporate Transformation* by Kilmann and Covin and develop a list of ideas to try out in my unit.

Books

Corporate Transformation: Revitalizing Organizations for a Competitive World by Ralph Kilmann and Teresa Covin. San Francisco: Jossey-Bass, 1988.

Change Agent Skills A: Assessing and Designing Excellence by Gerard Egan. Order through Pfeiffer & Co., 1-800-274-4434, Code #500ATI.

Change Agent Skills B: Managing Innovation and Change by Gerard Egan. Order through Pfeiffer & Co., 1-800-274-4434, Code #501ATI.

Intervention and Collaboration: Helping Organizations to Change by Hedley Dimock. Order through Pfeiffer & Co., 1-800-274-4434, Code #0361XAT1.

Managing Organizational Change by Cynthia Scott and Dennis Jaffe. Order through Crisp Publications. 1-800-442-7477. ISBN 0-931961-80-7.

Managing Beyond the Quick Fix by Ralph Kilmann. Jossey-Bass, 1989. Provides a high-level discussion of how to implement organizational change.

The Leadership Challenge by J. M. Kouzes & Barry Z. Posner. Code E76ATA, if ordered through Pfeiffer & Co., 1-800-274-4434.

Reengineering the Corporation by Michael Hammer and James Champy. New York: Harper Business, 1993.

Seminars and Workshops

The Learning Organization: A New Approach to Leading Your Company. Three days. American Management Association Course. Various locations. Tel. 518-891-0065. Mtg. No. 2503T23.

Facilitating Organizational Change. Two days. UA Consulting & Training Services. Various locations. Tel. 619-552-8901. Code: FOC-PC.

Effecting Change. Three days. Center for Creative Leadership. Tel. 336-545-2810.

Theories of Change Management. Five days. NTL Institute. Tel. 800-777-5227.

Creating Change for a Sustainable Environment. Five days. NTL Institute. Tel. 800-777-5227.

Leading Change. Three days. MasteryLab. Tel. 1-800-870-9490.

6. DEVELOPING OTHERS

Definition: The ability to delegate responsibility and to work with others and coach them to develop their capabilities.

An employee demonstrating this competency:

- Provides helpful, behaviorally specific feedback to others.
- Shares information, advice, and suggestions to help others to be more successful; provides effective coaching.
- Gives people assignments that will help develop their abilities.
- Regularly meets with employees to review their development progress.
- Recognizes and reinforces people's developmental efforts and improvements.
- Expresses confidence in others' ability to be successful.

Importance of this Competency

Developing Others helps an organization to get the most from its human resources. Employees with multiple skills can do more things and are more valuable to the organization. By developing others, an organization also cultivates people who can provide leadership. Many of the changes organizations try to implement (e.g., empowerment, self-directed work teams) require developing employee skills. This competency is also important because, in developing its employees, an organization demonstrates its commitment to its employees and thereby enhances motivation and productivity.

General Considerations in Developing this Competency

One of the challenges in developing this competency is giving it regular attention, often in the face of more pressing day-to-day problems. Managers who are strong at this competency make time for it; they schedule development planning meetings with employees at least quarterly. They look for opportunities that will develop their subordinates. To develop this competency, you will also need to develop skill at coaching. Many books and courses are available on this topic.

Practicing this Competency

Schedule regular development planning sessions with each employee.

Review your organization's performance management system to see how you can implement Developing Others within that system.

Ensure that each employee has an updated personal development plan.

Look for opportunities to assign your people to teams and projects that will develop their skills.

Involve your employees in planning and decision making to develop their skills in these areas.

Plan and implement training for your staff.

Recognize and praise behavior related to self development.

Obtaining Feedback

Periodically ask each of your employees for feedback on how you are implementing development planning and performance management. Ask for their ideas on how you can improve the process.

Learning from Experts

Interview someone who has a successful track record of developing staff. Ask what this person does, what has worked effectively and less effectively. Keep a list of ideas that you can apply with your own people.

Coaching Suggestions for Managers

If you are coaching someone who is trying to develop this competency, you can:

- Model the process of Developing Others in your own behavior with this person.
- Hold a session with this person to review what he/she has been doing to develop people.
- Recognize and praise behavior related to Developing Others.

Sample Development Goals

By December 12, I will meet with each of the people who report directly to me and begin the process of development planning.

By January 12, each of these employees will have a personal development plan.

By March 5, I will read *Performance Planning and Appraisal* by King, and develop a list of ideas to apply when coaching employees.

Books

Performance Planning and Appraisal by Patricia King. New York: McGraw-Hill, 1989.

Mentoring by Gordon Shea. Order through Crisp Publications. 1-800-442-7477. ISBN 0-931961-43-2.

The One-Minute Manager by Kenneth Blanchard and Spencer Johnson. New York: William Morrow, 1982.

Coaching: A Management Skill for Improving Individual Performance by Arthur Deegan. Reading, MA: Addison-Wesley, 1979.

Managing for Excellence: The Guide to Developing High Performance in Contemporary Organizations by David Bradford and Allan Cohen. New York: John Wiley and Sons, 1984.

The Lessons of Experience: How Successful Executives Develop on the Job by Morgan McCall, Michael Lombardo, and Ann Morrison. Lexington, MA: Lexington Books: 1988.

Seminars and Workshops

REACH™ Coaching Performance Excellence. Two days. MasteryLab. Tel. 1-800-870-9490.

Developing Value-Adding People and Adding Value (for employees). One-Two days each. MasteryLab. Tel. 1-800-870-9490

Managing Performance—With Competence. (Adding Value through PM.) Three days each. MasteryLab. Tel. 1-800-870-9490.

7. MANAGING PERFORMANCE

Definition: The ability to take responsibility for one's own or one's employees' performance by setting clear goals and expectations, tracking progress against the goals, ensuring feedback, and addressing performance problems and issues promptly.

Behaviors for employees:

- With his/her manager, sets specific, measurable goals that are realistic but challenging, with dates for accomplishment.
- With his/her manager, clarifies expectations about what will be done and how.
- Enlists his/her manager's support in obtaining the information, resources, and training needed to accomplish his/her work effectively.
- Promptly notifies his/her manager about any problems that affect his/her ability to accomplish planned goals.
- Seeks performance feedback from his/her manager and from others with whom he/she interacts on the job.
- Prepares a personal development plan with specific goals and a time line for their accomplishment.
- Takes significant action to develop skills needed for effectiveness in current or future job.

Behaviors for managers:

- Ensures that employees have clear goals and responsibilities.
- Works with employees to set and communicate performance standards that are specific and measurable.
- Supports employees in their efforts to achieve job goals (e.g., by providing resources, removing obstacles, acting as a buffer).
- Stays informed about employees' progress and performance through both formal methods (e.g., status reports) and informal methods (e.g., management by walking around).
- Provides specific performance feedback, both positive and corrective, as soon as possible after an event.
- Deals firmly and promptly with performance problems; lets people know what is expected of them and when.

Importance of this Competency

Managing Performance is a key competency for anyone supervising projects or people. By using this competency, supervisors provide direction, standards, and follow-up to ensure results. By managing performance, supervisors ensure that their unit achieves its goals. Additional benefits are happier and more productive employees.

General Considerations in Developing this Competency

This competency should be applied in the context of an organization's performance management system. Thus, if your organization has a system for performance management, a first step in developing this competency is to familiarize yourself with the forms and procedures of your organization's performance management system.

Although you can learn a great deal about performance management and prevent many mistakes by taking a course or reading books, this is a competency which requires learning by doing. If you are managing people, you have an opportunity to demonstrate Performance Management with each of your employees. The first step is to hold meetings with each employee to implement performance management. At these meetings, clarify the person's job responsibilities and the performance measures you will use to assess the person on each job responsibility. For many jobs it is useful to establish specific, measurable goals, with time lines for their accomplishment. In these discussions, it is important for the employee to have a two-way discussion with you to reach agreement on responsibilities, goals, and performance measurements. You should also set a date for a subsequent meeting to follow up on the employee's progress.

The next step is to establish formal or informal procedures for keeping track of employee progress. Regular meetings, reports, or voice mail communications are possible procedures.

This competency is closely related to several other competencies: Developing Others, Results Orientation, and Interpersonal Awareness. Review the sections on these competencies to identify ideas that will support your efforts to develop Managing Performance.

Practicing this Competency

Set up a meeting with each employee to plan his/her performance. Agree on responsibilities, performance measures, and a set of realistic but challenging goals with dates for their accomplishment.

Set up procedures by which employees can regularly report their progress and any obstacles they encounter.

Periodically visit each employee in his/her work area and ask about progress and issues. Check to see if employees have the resources and information they need in order to accomplish their tasks.

Keep a file for each employee in which you document accomplishments and performance problems.

Schedule regular performance planning meetings with each employee.

Provide specific behavioral feedback, both positive and corrective, as soon as possible after observing the behavior.

Address performance problems promptly.

Obtaining Feedback

Talk individually with each employee to get ideas on how you can better manage their performance.

If your company regularly administers an employee survey, check results that may indicate how you are doing as a manager. If your company does not administer a survey, or if the results cannot be analyzed to provide specific feedback to you from your employees, consider developing and administering a short survey that will allow them to provide anonymous feedback on your performance management. Include some open-ended questions asking for specific suggestions.

Learning from Experts

Interview someone strong in this competency. Ask for specific examples of what he/she has done that was effective in managing employee performance. Ask the person to talk about a time when he/she confronted a performance problem. Find out what the person said and why.

Coaching Suggestions for Managers

If you are coaching someone who is trying to develop this competency, you can:

• Model good performance management in your interactions with this person.
• Notice and praise behavior that indicates good performance management (e.g., holding regular performance management meetings).
• Encourage the person to discuss with you how he/she will confront performance issues with individual employees.

Sample Development Goals

By January 6, I will hold meetings with each employee to implement the first step in the company's performance management program.
By December 9, I will confront Randy regarding his leadership of the Design Team.
By February 22, I will provide some specific behavioral feedback about performance to each of my employees.
By March 8, I will read *Performance Planning and Appraisal* by King, and prepare a list of ideas that I can apply with my employees.

Books

Coaching for Commitment by Dennis Kinlaw. Order through Pfeiffer & Co., 1-800-274-4434, Code #527AT1.

Managing Performance by Marion Haynes. Order through Crisp Publications. 1-800-442-7477. ISBN 1-56052-017-5.

Performance Planning and Appraisal by Patricia King. New York: McGraw-Hill, 1989.

Delegating for Results by Robert Maddux. Order through Crisp Publications. 1-800-442-7477. ISBN 1-56052-008-6.

Handling the Difficult Employee by Marty Brownstein. Order through Crisp Publications. 1-800-442-7477. ISBN 1-56052-179-1.

Giving and Receiving Criticism by Patti Hathaway. Order through Crisp Publications. 1-800-442-7477. ISBN 1-56052-023-X.

Self-Study Courses

How to Plan and Conduct Productive Performance Appraisals. American Management Association Self-Study Course. 1-800-262-9699. Stock #94060CYI.

Dealing with Difficult Behavior. American Management Association Self-Study Course. 1-800-262-9699. Stock #80140CYI. Includes six audio cassettes.

Seminars and Workshops

Coaching and Counseling for Improved Job Performance. Three days. American Management Association Course. Various locations. Tel. 518-891-0065. Mtg. No. 2246TX5.

Managing Performance—With Competence. (Adding Value through PM.) Three days. MasteryLab. Tel. 1-800-870-9490.

REACH™ Coaching Performance Excellence. Two days. MasteryLab. Tel. 1-800-870-9490.

8. ATTENTION TO COMMUNICATION

Definition: The ability to ensure that information is passed on to others who should be kept informed.

An employee demonstrating this competency:

- Ensures that others involved in a project or effort are kept informed about developments and plans.
- Ensures that important information from his/her management is shared with his/her employees and others as appropriate.
- Shares ideas and information with others who might find them useful.
- Uses multiple channels or means to communicate important messages (e.g., memos, newsletters, meetings, electronic mail).
- Keeps his/her manager informed about progress and problems; avoids surprises.
- Ensures that regular, consistent communication takes place.

Importance of this Competency

Attention to Communication involves ensuring that important information gets to those who must have it. This competency is especially important to leaders, because leaders must ensure that everyone in the organization understands the overall direction and that the efforts of different groups are aligned with each other and with the overall plans. Attention to Communication is also important when groups from different organizations must coordinate their activities (e.g., sales should alert manufacturing about potential contracts).

General Considerations in Developing this Competency

This competency does not require significant development of new skills. What is needed is appreciation of the importance of ensuring good communication. Putting the competency into practice involves creating vehicles for communication (e.g., regular meetings, project newsletters; mailing lists to be used with voice mail) and ensuring that communication takes place.

In formulating the communications, other communication competencies are important: Oral Communication, Written Communication, and Persuasive Communication. As in all communication, it is important to ensure that communications are clear, concise, and addressed to the needs of the audience.

Practicing this Competency

Identify all the groups with which your unit should be communicating on a regular basis. Consider the existing processes and vehicles for communication and how they are used. Identify and implement ways to improve the frequency and quality of communication.

Investigate and implement ways to use information technology to improve communication in your work group (e.g., implementing voice mail; creating mailing lists for voice mail; using e-mail; adopting software programs for group work).

If you are part of a team responsible for disseminating information to the organization, meet with the team to discuss alternative ways to do this. Try several different methods and solicit feedback about the effectiveness of each method. Important messages should be communicated repeatedly and in different ways.

If you are part of a cross-functional team, set up one-to-one meetings with individuals from different parts of the organization to let them know what your team is doing and to solicit feedback and ideas.

Obtaining Feedback

After sending out a significant report or memo, contact people and ask for feedback on it. Try to find out how many people read and remembered it and what they thought of it.

If you use voice mail or e-mail as part of your work, ask coworkers how effectively you use these communication vehicles and what you can do to improve your effectiveness in communicating.

Learning from Experts

Observe the communication behavior of a skilled leader. Look at the frequency, style, and format of this person's communications. If possible, ask this person about his/her thinking in planning particular communications.

Before sending out an important communication, ask for suggestions from someone strong in communication skills.

Coaching Suggestions for Managers

If you are coaching someone who is trying to develop this competency, you can:

- Model this competency by sharing information and by crafting clear, concise messages addressing the needs of the audience.
- Provide assignments that involve drafting memos, reports, or other communications. Provide constructive feedback on the communications.
- Help this person think through the communication vehicles and messages needed by a unit or team of which he/she is a part.
- Assign this person to a team or task force headed by someone who demonstrates a high level of attention to communication.

Sample Development Goals

By June 12, I will make recommendations to the Planning Team on ways we should communicate the new operational plan to the division.

By July 1, I will distribute a memo to all division members summarizing the work of the Waste Reduction Team. A week later, I will call six of the department heads and ask for feedback on this memo.

Books

Flip Charts: How to Draw Them and How to Use Them by Richard Brandt. Order through Pfeiffer & Co., 1-800-274-4434, Code #544C34.

The Leadership Challenge by J. M. Kouzes & Barry Z. Posner. Especially pp. 56–60, 118–124, 205–210. Code E76ATA, if ordered through Pfeiffer & Co., 1-800-274-4434.

Self-Study Courses

Communication Skills for Managers. American Management Association Self-Study Course. Tel. 1-800-262-9699. Stock #95047CYI.

Seminars and Workshops

Communicating for Maximum Results. Three days. American Management Association Course. Various locations. Tel. 518-891-0065. Code 2235TPD.

Communication and Interpersonal Skills. Three days. American Management Association Course. Various locations. Tel. 518-891-0065. Code 2576TPD.

9. ORAL COMMUNICATION

Definition: The ability to express oneself clearly in conversations and interactions with others.

An employee demonstrating this competency:

- Speaks clearly and can be easily understood.
- Tailors the content of speech to the level and experience of the audience.
- Uses appropriate grammar and choice of words in oral speech.
- Organizes ideas clearly in oral speech.
- Expresses ideas concisely in oral speech.
- Maintains eye contact when speaking with others.
- Summarizes or paraphrases his/her understanding of what others have said to verify understanding and prevent miscommunication.

Importance of this Competency

For many tasks, oral communication is the most frequent and most important means of communication. We use oral communication to express and explain ideas, to ask questions, engage in discussion, seek support, negotiate, make presentations, and leave voice mail messages. Even if your job involves extensive written or graphic communication, your ability to express your ideas orally is probably very important to your effectiveness. As more work is done by teams, oral communication will become even more important.

Oral Communication includes several related abilities:

- Speaking clearly enough so that others can understand your words (e.g., without mumbling, slurring words, or speaking with a heavy accent).
- Speaking logically, so that others can follow your reasoning.
- Using appropriate grammar and vocabulary, that do not detract from your credibility.
- Maintaining and directing the flow of a dialogue (e.g., by paraphrasing what the other person has said to verify one's understanding).

General Considerations in Developing this Competency

Developing this competency is like learning a new sport. If you were starting to play tennis, you might look for opportunities to play, but you would probably not show significant improvement until you found a coach who could give you specific instructions, observe you trying to follow these instructions, and provide feedback and suggestions for improvement. To develop oral communication skills, you also need instruction, opportunity for practice, and constructive feedback. You can find these components in courses on public speaking and presentation skills. You can also learn by getting coaching and feedback from your manager or another coworker.

Practicing this Competency

Practice speaking clearly, without mumbling.

Before a meeting or presentation, think about the background of your audience. What examples can you use that would be familiar to this audience? What technical terms or jargon should you avoid using because they will be unfamiliar to the audience?

Before a meeting or other situation where you plan to express your ideas, write them down on paper and find a clear way to organize them.

Practice maintaining eye contact during conversations to show that you are attentive and interested.

During a conversation, periodically summarize or paraphrase what the other person has said to verify your understanding, e.g., "You have expressed three concerns: (1) that the new product will have to be priced at a level that won't be competitive, (2) that the development process is likely to take much longer than eight months, and (3) that the sales staff may not understand and support it. Have I captured your concerns accurately?"

Look for opportunities to express ideas orally or to make presentations. Plan what you will say and evaluate your effectiveness in saying it.

Obtaining Feedback

Before a meeting or presentation in which you plan to express yourself orally, ask someone to observe you and give you constructive suggestions on how you can express yourself more effectively.

During a presentation or meeting at which you are expressing ideas, if you see nonverbal signs that people are not keeping up with you, stop to check for understanding (e.g., "Are you following me?"). Then, if necessary, explain your ideas again in a different way.

Learning from Experts

Listen carefully to someone skilled in oral communication. Notice how the person introduces his/her talk and how he/she communicates the organization of ideas. Pay attention to the choice of examples and stories. Observe the person's pace, gestures, and animation.

Coaching Suggestions for Managers

If you are coaching someone who is trying to develop this competency, you can:

- Model good oral communication.
- Provide specific suggestions and constructive feedback.
- Notice and praise improvements in oral communication.
- Provide opportunities for training in public speaking and presentation skills.

Sample Development Goals

By October 8, I will make an oral presentation of my competitive analysis to the Product Development Team. Before the presentation, I will outline my ideas and get feedback from Rob Sanders. After the presentation, I will ask for feedback on the presentation from Judy Johnson and Mike Babbitt.

During the week of October 7–11, I will maintain eye contact at least 80 percent of the time in all conversations at work.

By December 18, I will complete a course on presentation skills.

Books

How to Talk So People Listen by Sonya Hamlin. Order through Association for Quality and Participation, 1-513-381-2959. HR06P.

Quick & Easy Way to Effective Speaking by Dale Carnegie, PB, 1990.

Making Successful Presentations: A Self-Teaching Guide by Terry Smith. New York: Wiley, 1984. Code G90AA, if ordered through Pfeiffer & Co., 1-800-274-4434.

Self-Study Courses

Word Power: How to Build Your Vocabulary. American Management Association Self-Study Course. 1-800-262-9699. Stock #94082CYI.

Seminars and Workshops

Effective Executive Speaking. American Management Association Course. Three days. Various locations. Tel. 518-891-0065. Mtg. No. 2522TX5.

Successful Communication. Two days. American Management Association Course. Various locations. Tel. 518-891-0065. Mtg. No. 2286UAC.

Presentations that Work. Booher Consultants, Inc. Two days. Tel. 805-563-7731.

10. WRITTEN COMMUNICATION

Definition: The ability to express oneself clearly in business writing.

An employee demonstrating this competency:

- Expresses ideas clearly and concisely in writing.
- Organizes written ideas clearly and signals the organization to the reader (e.g., through an introductory paragraph or through use of headings).
- Tailors written communications to effectively reach an audience.
- Uses graphics and other aids to clarify complex or technical information.
- Spells correctly.
- Writes using concrete, specific language.
- Uses punctuation correctly.
- Writes grammatically.
- Uses an appropriate business writing style.

Importance of this Competency

Written Communication is used in business letters, instructions, technical manuals, proposals, contracts, and performance appraisals. When information is important enough to be documented, written communication is used. Only a minority of workers use this competency extensively, but most workers must be able to use it effectively for selected situations.

General Considerations in Developing this Competency

Like Oral Communication, Written Communication is best developed through deliberate instruction, feedback, and coaching. This kind of instruction is available in courses on business writing and may also be provided by managers or coworkers willing to work with someone to develop his/her writing skills.

If your writing skills need refinement rather than significant development, you may benefit from reviewing books on business writing and from applying some of the practice ideas suggested below.

Practicing this Competency

Prepare and revise an outline of your ideas before writing an initial draft.

Use formats that clearly convey the organization of your ideas (e.g., different levels of headings, bulleting or numbering of key points).

For documents longer than one page, set forth the broad organization in an initial paragraph or section.

Review and revise your initial draft until you are satisfied with it. Look for ways to simplify your communications and make them more concise.

Consider the level and experience of your audience and select examples accordingly.

Consider adding graphics to make your written communications more interesting.

Use the spell checker and grammar checker on your computer.

For effective formatting of presentations, use a template in one of the many excellent presentation software programs.

Obtaining Feedback

Have someone whose judgment you trust review your written communications and suggest revisions before you send them out. Distribute a copy of a presentation you plan to deliver and ask for feedback and suggestions.

Learning from Experts

Look for opportunities to work with skilled writers to co-author written communications. Find and study good examples of the kind of written communications you need to prepare: business letters, contracts, proposals, or presentations. Note the organization and format.

Coaching Suggestions for Managers

If you are coaching someone who is trying to develop this competency, you can:

• Provide assignments that require preparing written communications.
• Work with this person to plan and outline a written communication. Discuss the reasons for a particular organization, format, and content.
• Carefully review and suggest revisions on written communications. Have the person implement the revisions.
• Provide assignments requiring this person to work closely with a skilled writer to help prepare written communications.
• Steer this person to a course on business writing.

Sample Development Goals

By March 30, I will prepare a written proposal to develop a video on team participation skills.
By March 10, I will meet with Sally Reimer to outline the proposal's contents.
By March 17, I will prepare a first draft.
By March 20, I will meet with Jim Deedan to get feedback and suggestions.
By March 30, I will complete the final revised draft.
By April 30, I will complete a course on business writing skills.

Books

How to Write Easily and Effectively. American Management Association. Order through AMA, 1-800-262-9699, Order #7641TPD.

Persuasive Business Proposals by Tom Sant. American Management Association. Order through AMA, 1-800-262-9699, Order #5100TPD.

Make Yourself Clear: Improving Business Communication by John O. Morris. New York: McGraw Hill, 1980.

Self-Study Courses

The Grammar and Proofreading Course. American Management Association Self-Study Course. 1-800-262-9699. Stock #94086CYI.

Fundamentals of Business Writing. American Management Association Self-Study Course. 1-800-262-9699. Stock #95067CYI.

How to Sharpen Your Business Writing Skills. American Management Association Self-Study Course. 1-800-262-9699. Stock #95042CYI.

Seminars and Workshops

How to Sharpen Your Business Writing Skills. Four days. American Management Association Course. Various locations. Tel. 518-891-0065. Mtg. No. 2516TX5.

Effective Writing Workshop. Booher Consultants, Inc. Two days. Tel. 805-563-7731.

11. PERSUASIVE COMMUNICATION

Definition: The ability to plan and deliver oral and written communications that make an impact and persuade their intended audiences.

An employee demonstrating this competency:

- Identifies and presents information or data that will have a strong effect on others.
- Selects language and examples tailored to the level and experience of the audience.
- Selects stories, analogies, or examples to illustrate a point.
- Creates graphics, overheads, or slides that display information clearly and with high impact.
- Presents several different arguments in support of a position.

Importance of this Competency

Persuasive Communication is important for professionals in sales and marketing. It is also important for leaders who need to gain support for a new vision of the organization, for an operational plan, and for changes in structure and work processes. This competency is also important for anyone who wants to gain others' support for initiatives.

General Considerations in Developing this Competency

This competency involves developing two skills. The first of these is designing and developing communications that will have a persuasive impact. This skill requires thinking about and anticipating the impact of various communication strategies. Two kinds of information can be used to achieve a persuasive impact: (1) identifying and highlighting arguments or data that are logically compelling and (2) identifying and highlighting arguments or data that address specific interests, concerns, or fears of the audience.

An excellent way to enhance your ability to design and develop persuasive communications is to work closely with someone who is skilled in this ability. Books and courses on presentation skills can also be helpful.

The second skill involved in Persuasive Communication is presentation delivery. A course in presentation skills is likely to be especially helpful because it combines specific instruction with practice and feedback. There also are books, videos, and self-study courses to develop presentation skills.

Practicing this Competency

Look for and take advantage of opportunities to prepare and deliver presentations.

In designing a presentation, identify and highlight information that will have a persuasive impact because it is logically compelling.

In designing a presentation or preparing for an influence meeting, try to anticipate the interests and concerns of the audience. Before the meeting or presentation, call someone in the audience and ask what kind of information would be most helpful and what the audience will be most interested in hearing.

In constructing a presentation, use examples or analogies based on the experience of your audience. For example, if you are talking to your manufacturing staff, you might use examples dealing with production runs.

Take time to find and develop interesting stories to illustrate points in a presentation.

Use presentation software to develop attractive, high-impact graphics for your presentation.

Obtaining Feedback

Before delivering a presentation, review the content with someone whose judgment you trust and ask for feedback and suggestions.

Ask someone to observe you delivering a presentation and to give you feedback and constructive suggestions.

Have someone videotape you delivering or rehearsing a presentation. Then view the video and note specific things you can do to improve your presentation delivery.

Learning from Experts

Observe someone skilled in creating and delivering presentations. Note the content and organization of the presentation. What ideas could you use in your presentations. Study the person's delivery of the presentation. Note the person's verbal and nonverbal behavior. What does this person do that you could do in your presentations?

Coaching Suggestions for Managers

If you are coaching someone who is trying to develop this competency, you can:

- Provide opportunities for this person to observe skilled presenters. Discuss what the person noticed in the skilled presenter's presentations.
- Help the person plan the organization and content of a presentation. Share the reasons underlying your thinking.
- Observe the person deliver a presentation and provide specific, constructive feedback, both positive and negative.
- If you are managing several persons who have opportunities to give presentations, debrief each presentation and ensure that each person receives useful, constructive feedback.
- Provide opportunities for presentation skills training.

Sample Development Goals

By June 10, I will read *How to Present Like a Pro* by Lani Arredondo, and identify a list of ideas to build into my presentation at the Western Marketing Region Meeting.

By June 5, I will have Cindy Spier videotape me rehearsing a presentation, and I will ask her to provide feedback and suggestions for improvement.

By July 10, I will learn to use Microsoft Powerpoint to prepare a sales presentation to Omega Company.

By July 25, I will complete a course on presentation skills.

Books

Effective Presentation Skills by Steve Mandel. Order through Crisp Publications. 1-800-442-7477. ISBN 1-56-52-202-X.

How to Present Like a Pro: Getting People to See Things Your Way by Lani Arredondo. New York: McGraw-Hill, 1991.

Making Successful Presentations: A Self-Teaching Guide by Terry Smith. New York: Wiley, 1984. Code G90ATA, if ordered through Pfeiffer & Co., Tel. 1-800-274-4434.

The Quick and Easy Way to Effective Public Speaking by Dale and Dorothy Carnegie. New York: Associated Press Pocket Books, 1977.

Persuasive Business Presentations by N. Robinson. Code M053ATA, if ordered through Pfeiffer & Co., Tel. 1-800-274-4434.

I Can See You Naked by Ron Hoff. Kansas City, Mo.: Andrews & McMeel, 1992.

Self-Study Courses

How to Deliver Winning Presentations. American Management Association Self-Study Course. 1-800-262-9699. Stock #94017CYI.

How to Speak Persuasively. American Management Association Self-Study Course. 1-800-262-9699. Stock #94095CYI.

Seminars and Workshops

Strategies for Developing Effective Presentation Skills. Three days. American Management Association Course. Various locations. Tel. 518-891-0065. Mtg No. 2519T23.

Effective Executive Speaking. Three days. American Management Association Course. Various locations. Tel. 518-891-0065. Mtg. No. 2522T23.

Peak Dynamics. Two days. Theatre Techniques for Business People. Tel. 770-216-9339.

12. INTERPERSONAL AWARENESS

Definition: The ability to notice, interpret, and anticipate others' concerns and feelings, and to communicate this awareness empathetically to others.

An employee demonstrating this competency:

- Understands the interests and important concerns of others.
- Notices and accurately interprets what others are feeling, based on their choice of words, tone of voice, expressions, and other nonverbal behavior.
- Anticipates how others will react to a situation.
- Listens attentively to people's ideas and concerns.
- Understands both the strengths and weaknesses of others.
- Understands the unspoken meaning in a situation.
- Says or does things to address others' concerns.
- Finds non-threatening ways to approach others about sensitive issues.
- Makes others feel comfortable by responding in ways that convey interest in what they have to say.

Importance of this Competency

Interpersonal Awareness is a fundamental interpersonal skill. It has two key aspects: (1) noticing what people are feeling, especially when they are not stating their feelings explicitly, and (2) showing by your responses to others that you care about their concerns. Interpersonal awareness is essential in influencing, selling, team leadership, and people management. If you are aware of other people's concerns, interests, and feelings, you are in a position to address them and, in so doing, to gain people's support for what you would like to accomplish.

General Considerations in Developing this Competency

Interpersonal Awareness often comes naturally to people who are "people-oriented;" other people may need special effort and training. One challenge in learning this competency is to overcome the tendency to focus so heavily on your own needs and concerns that you miss the signals being sent nonverbally by other people. Another challenge is to show by the tone and content of your response that you care about the other person's concerns.

The skills related to Interpersonal Awareness are easiest to develop in a course that provides opportunities for observation, practice, and role playing. If your interpersonal awareness skills need significant development, you should enroll in a course on listening skills. If you need only minor enhancement of your skills, you may be able to learn from some of the readings and practice suggestions.

Practicing this Competency

Practice by using these basic listening skills:

- Listen with full attention.
- Make responsive comments that show empathy (e.g., "That must have been really frustrating," or "You must have been upset"). Use a tone of voice appropriate to the emotion.

- Periodically summarize what the other person has said to let the other person know that you have heard what he/she has said.
- Avoid judgmental comments (e.g., "You should have known better than to do that").
- Avoid giving advice.
- Be open to feedback, both verbal and nonverbal, that indicates that you have missed other people's concerns.

Find opportunities to talk individually and informally with your clients, customers and coworkers. Ask them what parts of their jobs are going well and what parts are more difficult. Ask about their personal interests outside of work. Use these conversations as opportunities to learn about the other person's interests, concerns, and aspirations.

Practice demonstrating empathy by describing and reflecting back the feelings that you are perceiving in others, using a tone of voice that shows understanding and appreciation for the feelings of the other person.

If you are managing people, make a point of checking in with each one daily. Ask how things are going and give your people an opportunity to talk about any concerns they may have.

Obtaining Feedback

Ask coworkers or friends to observe you and provide feedback to you over a two-week period on the responsiveness and interpersonal sensitivity that you demonstrate. Ask them to let you know when you seem genuinely interested and responsive and when you seem insensitive.

Learning from Experts

Observe someone with a reputation for strong interpersonal skills. Note this person's verbal and nonverbal behavior in interpersonal situations, especially difficult situations involving selling, influencing, counseling, or dealing with someone who is upset.

Coaching Suggestions for Managers

If you are coaching someone who is trying to develop this competency, you can:

- Model listening skills, responsiveness, and sensitivity in your interactions with this person.
- Agree to observe this person and provide feedback on Interpersonal Awareness.
- Discuss and share your thoughts about how you will approach delicate interpersonal situations (e.g., interactions with customers or vendors).
- Set and enforce norms in your work group for listening to others and treating them with respect.

Sample Development Goals

By February 10, I will read *Listening: The Forgotten Skill* by Madelyn Burley-Allen, and prepare a list of ideas to practice.

By March 15, I will meet with each of the people who report to me to get to know them better. I will ask them what they like and dislike in their work, what their personal interests are, and what I can do to help them become more effective.

By May 31, I will complete a course on listening skills.

Books

The Business of Listening by Diana Bonet. Order through Crisp Publications. 1-800-442-7477. ISBN 1-56052-286-0.

Listening: The Forgotten Skill by Madelyn Burley-Allen. New York: Wiley, 1982. Code HO5ATA, if ordered through Pfeiffer & Co., Tel. 1-800-274-4434.

How to Listen—How to Be Heard by Thomas Banville. Nelson-Hall, 1978.

The Seven Habits of Highly Effective People by Stephen Covey. Especially Habit 5: Seek First to Understand, then to be Understood. Can be ordered through Covey Leadership Center, 1-800-553-8889.

Self-Study Courses

Listen and Be Listened to. American Management Association Self-Study Course. 1-800-262-9699. Stock #80204CYI. Includes four audio cassettes.

Seminars and Workshops

AMA's Course on Interpersonal Skills. Three days. American Management Association Course. Various locations. Tel. 518-891-0065. Mtg. No. 2575T23.

The ParTraining Corporation and its affiliates offer an excellent one-day course on listening skills and a three-day program that includes listening skills and influence skills. 1-800-247-7188.

Management Work Conference. Five days. NTL Institute. Various locations. Tel. 800-777-5227.

REACH™ Coaching Performance Excellence. Two days. MasteryLab. Tel. 1-800-870-9490.

Other Resources

The Seven Habits of Highly Effective People by Stephen Covey. Six audio cassettes. Order through Nightingale Conant, 1-800-525-9000. Code #786PAS.

How to Become an Effective Listener by Tony Alessandra. 45-minute video. Order through Talico, Tel. 904-241-1721. Code TI 203.

13. INFLUENCING OTHERS

Definition: The ability to gain others' support for ideas, proposals, projects, and solutions.

An employee demonstrating this competency:

- Presents arguments that address others' most important concerns and issues and looks for win-win solutions.
- Involves others in a process or decision to ensure their support.
- Offers trade-offs or exchanges to gain commitment.
- Identifies and proposes solutions that benefit all parties involved in a situation.
- Enlists experts or third parties to influence others.
- Develops other indirect strategies to influence others.
- Knows when to escalate critical issues to own or others' management, if own efforts to enlist support have not succeeded.
- Structures situations (e.g., the setting, persons present, sequence of events) to create a desired impact and to maximize the chances of a favorable outcome.
- Works to make a particular impression on others.
- Identifies and targets influence efforts at the real decision makers and those who can influence them.
- Seeks out and builds relationships with others who can provide information, intelligence, career support, potential business, and other forms of help.
- Takes a personal interest in others (e.g., by asking about their concerns, interests, family, friends, hobbies) to develop relationships.
- Accurately anticipates the implications of events or decisions for various stakeholders in the organization and plans strategy accordingly.

Importance of this Competency

This competency, which is the ability to get others to do what you would like them to do, is fundamental to many goals and activities at work: selling, enlisting support for ideas, obtaining resources, motivating subordinates, energizing teams, and building support for an organizational vision. The higher your level in an organization, the more important is this competency.

More and more organizations are moving away from hierarchical structures, in which influence depends heavily on the use of positional power. The increasing use of teams requires influence skills, rather than authority, to gain support.

General Considerations in Developing this Competency

As the behaviors for this competency show, there are many ways to demonstrate this competency. Most of these involve careful analysis of the needs, interests, concerns, and fears of the persons to be influenced. Based on this analysis, the skillful influencer considers alternative approaches and develops influence strategies. The strategies reflect thinking that is not always shown in observable behavior. Developing this competency requires learning this kind of thinking.

One of the best methods to develop Influencing Others is to work closely with someone skilled in developing influence strategies. Another method is to learn about influence strategies through courses and books. Using influence strategies effectively requires practice and feedback. Courses that involve role playing and feedback can provide this practice.

This competency builds on several other competencies, especially Interpersonal Awareness and Persuasive Communication. Developing these competencies will help develop Influencing Others. In addition, Influencing Others often requires knowing or learning about the politics of an organization: the histories and agendas of different groups and the decision makers and key influencers of particular types of decisions.

Practicing this Competency

The next time you need to influence someone, ask that person or others what are his/her most important needs and concerns.

Try to think of a solution that will address the other person's needs or concerns while meeting your own objectives.

Consider involving others by asking for input, checking out possible approaches, or working with them to develop a plan to gain their support.

Think about what you can offer the other person or group in exchange for what you would like from this person or group.

Try to think of solutions that will benefit everyone involved in a situation. The book *Getting to Yes* by Roger Fisher and William Ury provides many useful ideas for doing this.

If an issue is critical and you have exhausted other approaches, consider escalating the issue to your own manager or the other person's manager. This is a strategy that should be used only when absolutely necessary, since it often provokes negative reactions in the other person.

Before a meeting at which it is important to gain the support of another person or group consider what you can do to structure the event (e.g., by orchestrating the setting, attendees, sequence of events, refreshments, entertainment) to achieve a desired outcome.

To influence a decision in your own organization or a client's, try to learn who the decision makers are and what their concerns are likely to be. Try to talk directly to the real decision makers.

To build a basis for influence efforts in the future, develop and maintain relationships with others from whom you may need support. Find ways to help them. Try to learn about their interests and concerns.

Obtaining Feedback

Before implementing an influence strategy, discuss it with others and ask for their feedback and suggestions.

After an interaction in which you tried to enlist the support of an individual or group, ask a colleague who was present for feedback and suggestions on your influence efforts.

Learning from Experts

Look for opportunities to work closely on tasks requiring the development of influence strategies (e.g., planning a presentation or sales call, leading a group to achieve a particular outcome).

Observe a skilled influencer using influence skills in situations such as sales calls, speeches, meetings with subordinates, and meetings to build relationships. Notice what the person says, how he/she says it, and the verbal and nonverbal reactions of the persons present.

Interview a skilled influencer about times when this person successfully influenced others. Try to get the sequence of what the person did and thought. Recognize that the person you interview may be reluctant to discuss some influence efforts, particularly those used to influence the person's current supervisor.

Coaching Suggestions for Managers

If you are coaching someone who is trying to develop this competency, you can:

- Involve this person in some of your own influence efforts and share your thinking about your goals, plans, and the reasons underlying them.
- Provide assignments requiring the use of influence skills; e.g., developing a presentation to senior management or planning a meeting with another group whose cooperation is needed. Provide suggestions and feedback on the planning and implementation of influence strategies.
- Provide opportunities for this person to work closely with skilled influencers.

Sample Development Goals

By September 10, I will read *Getting to Yes* by Fisher and Ury and use what I learn to develop a strategy for gaining the cooperation of the R&D Division.

By November 3, I will hold meetings to build relationships with five individuals from other departments whose support I may need over the coming year.

Before the October 5 sales meeting with Central Information, I will call the two project managers they are inviting to that meeting to learn what they would like to gain from the meeting. I will then plan and deliver a presentation that addresses these needs and interests.

By December 15, I will complete a course on Influencing Others.

Books

Getting Things Done When You are Not in Charge by Geoffrey Bellman. Order through Pfeiffer & Co., 1-800-274-4434, Code #H75C34.

Influencing Others by William Nothstine. Order through Crisp Publications. 1-800-442-7477. ISBN 0-931961-84-X.

Influence Without Authority by Allen Cohen and David Bradford. Order through Association for Quality and Participation, 1-513-381-1959. WL10P.

Getting to Yes: Negotiating Agreement Without Giving In by Roger Fisher and William Ury. Penguin Books, 1983.

Getting Past No: Negotiating Your Way from Confrontation to Cooperation by William Ury. New York: Bantam Books, 1991.

You Can Negotiate Anything by Herb Cohen. New York: Bantam, 1990.

The Empowered Manager: Positive Political Skills at Work by Peter Block. San Francisco: Jossey-Bass, 1989.

The Seven Habits of Highly Effective People by Stephen Covey Especially Habit 4: Think Win/Win. Order through Covey Leadership Center, 1-800-553-8889.

Is Your "Net" Working? A Complete Guide to Building Contacts and Career Visibility by Anne Boe and Bettie Young. Wiley, 1989.

Power and Influence: Beyond the Final Authority by John Kotter. Free Press, 1985.

Consultative Selling: The Human Formula for High Margin Sales at High Levels by Mack Hanan. AMACOM, 1990.

Self-Study Courses

Successful Negotiating. American Management Association Self-Study Course. 1-800-262-9699. Stock #95024CYI.

Interpersonal Negotiations. American Management Association Self-Study Course. 1-800-262-9699. Stock #95053CYI.

How to Negotiate. American Management Association Self-Study Course. 1-800-262-9699. Stock #801332CYI. Includes six audio cassettes.

Consultative Selling. American Management Association Self-Study Course. 1-800-262-9699. Stock #80200CYI. Includes four audio cassettes.

Value Selling: How to Sell to Cost-Conscious Customers. American Management Association Self-Study Course. 1-800-262-9699. Stock #80194CYI. Includes four audio cassettes.

How to Deal with Differences in People by Tony Alessandra. Six audio cassettes plus Progress Guide and Behavioral-Style Evaluation. Order through Nightingale Conant, 1-800-525-9000. Code 1431AS.

Negotiating Strategies for the Real World by William Ury. Six audio cassettes plus workbook. Order through Nightingale Conant, 1-800-525-9000. Code 691AS.

Seminars and Workshops

Negotiating to Win. Three days. American Management Association Course. Various locations. Tel. 518-891-0065. Mtg. No. 2513T23.

Leadership and Teamwork. Three days. ParTraining Corporation and its affiliates. 1-800-247-7188.

EXTEND™ Consulting Skills. Two days. MasteryLab. Tel. 1-800-870-9490.

Team Selling and SalesPro™. Three days. MasteryLab. Tel. 1-800-870-9490.

Power Negotiating. Three days. MasteryLab. Tel. 1-800-870-9490.

Positive Power and Influence—Situation Management Systems. Tel. 617-826-4433.

Influencing Effectively. Five days. NTL Institute. Tel. 800-777-5227.

Other Resources

How to Gain Power and Influence with People by Tony Alessandra. Six audio cassettes. Order through Nightingale Conant, 1-800-525-9000. Code 370AS.

The Seven Habits of Highly Effective People by Stephen Covey. Six audio cassettes. Order through Nightingale Conant, 1-800-525-9000. Code786PAS.

The Art of Influencing People Positively by Tony Alessandra. 45-minute video. Order through Talico, Tel. 904-241-1721. Code TI-201.

14. BUILDING COLLABORATIVE RELATIONSHIPS

Definition: The ability to develop, maintain, and strengthen partnerships with others inside or outside the organization, who can provide information, assistance, and support.

An employee demonstrating this competency:

- Asks about the other person's personal experience, interests, and family.
- Asks questions to identify shared interests, experiences, or other common ground.
- Shows an interest in what others have to say; acknowledges their perspectives and ideas.
- Recognizes the business concerns and perspectives of others.
- Expresses gratitude and appreciation to others who have provided information, assistance, or support.
- Takes time to get to know coworkers, to build rapport and establish a common bond.
- Tries to build relationships with people whose assistance, cooperation, and support may be needed.
- Provides assistance, information, and support to others to build a basis for future reciprocity.

Importance of This Competency

This competency is important for people whose effectiveness depends on building partnerships with others inside or outside the organization. Building Collaborative Relationships is important in large organizations, especially politicized ones, in which people are reluctant to lend support to others whom they do not know and trust. This competency is also very important to sales representatives who need to make repeated sales to the same individual or organization and who need to make sales requiring the support of many players.

Building Collaborative Relationships is closely related to two other competencies—Interpersonal Awareness and Influencing Others.

General Considerations in Developing This Competency

To develop this competency, you must (1) realize its importance, (2) practice the behaviors, and (3) develop relevant skills. To appreciate the importance of this competency, consult readings, especially ones on power and influence. It is also helpful to talk to people skilled at relationship building. Practicing the behaviors requires setting up meetings with people who can provide assistance or support. The relevant skills involve listening, influencing, and negotiating. Thus, in addition to reviewing the suggestions below for this competency, you may want to review the sections on two other competencies: Interpersonal Awareness and Influencing Others.

Practicing This Competency

Make a chart to use to assess and track your business relationship building. In one column, list the names of people with whom it is important for you to build good relationships. In the second column, note the type of information or assistance each person can potentially provide. In the third column write a number assessing the current state of that relationship:

−1= negative relationship characterized by hostility and distrust.
　0= no relationship. You don't know the other person.
　1= acquaintance. You know the person and are cordial to each other.
　2= positive relationship. You have provided significant assistance or support to each other.
　3= strong positive relationship. Besides providing significant assistance to each other, you see each other socially and have full trust in each other.

Target several persons with whom you would like to establish a better working relationship. Set up an informal meeting with each person, in which you

- Take time to develop rapport by sharing information about personal interests and family activities.
- Ask about the other person's business objectives and concerns.
- Show interest and concern for what the other person is experiencing.
- Suggest ways that you may be able to help support this person.

Think of everyone who has provided assistance or support to you over the past month or two. Write a note to each person expressing your appreciation.

Explain some of your business goals and interests to several people with whom you have a relationship and ask these people who else you might speak with to help further your goals. Set up meetings with these individuals and begin the process of relationship building.

Learning from Experts

Interview several individuals who are skilled at developing business relationships. Ask them to talk about several relationships they have established with coworkers, vendors, or customers, and to describe

- How they initially established the relationship.
- What they have done to maintain the relationship.
- How they have helped the other person.
- How the other person has helped them.
- What approaches have been most effective for them in building business relationships.

Coaching Suggestions for Managers

If you are coaching someone who is trying to develop this competency, you can:

- Model the process by bringing this person to meetings you have set up to maintain a business relationship or to meetings you have set up to develop new business relationships.
- Arrange for the person to meet and attempt to build relationships with people with whom you have already developed relationships.
- Ask the person to meet with you after a relationship-building meeting to discuss what happened and to provide suggestions.
- Observe and provide feedback on the person's relationship-building activities.

Sample Development Goals

By January 15, I will interview Curt Bond about his experiences in relationship building.

By February 10, I will read Part III of *The Seven Habits of Highly Effective People* by Stephen Covey.

By March 1, I will set up meetings with Mary Rainmaker, Nace Ayer, and Joan Blocker to discuss goals and perspectives and establish working relationships.

Books

The Seven Habits of Highly Effective People by Stephen Covey. Especially Habits 4 and 5. Order through Covey Leadership Center, 1-800-553-8889.

General Managers by John Kotter. Free Press, 1986.

Influence Without Authority by Allen Cohen and David Bradford. Order through Association for Quality and Participation, 1-513-381-1959. WL10P.

Getting To Yes, Negotiating Agreement Without Giving In by Roger Fisher and William Ury. Penguin Books, 1983.

Is Your "Net" Working? A Complete Guide to Building Contacts and Career Visibility by Anne Boe and Bettie Young. Wiley, 1989.

Managing With People: Politics and Influence in Organizations by Jeffrey Pfeffer. Boston: Harvard Business School Press, 1992. See especially Chapter 9.

Networking: How to Enrich Your Life and Get Things Done by Donald R. Woods and Shirley D. Ormerod. Order through Pfeiffer & Co., 1-800-272-4434, Code 03636C34.

Power and Influence: Beyond the Final Authority by John Kotter. Wiley, 1985.

Self-Study Courses

Relationship Strategies: How to Deal with Differences in People by Tony Alessandra. Six audio cassettes plus Progress Guide and Behavioral-Style Evaluation. Order through Nightingale Conant, 1-800-525-9000. Code 1431AS.

Seminars and Workshops

Leadership and Team Work. Three days. ParTraining Corporation and its affiliates. 1-800-247-7188.

Building Interdepartmental Cooperation. Three days. American Management Association. Various locations. Course #2505UNR. 1-800-262-9699.

EXTEND™ Consulting Skills. Two days. MasteryLab. Tel. 1-800-870-9490.

Other Resources

The Seven Habits of Highly Effective People by Stephen Covey. Six audio cassettes. Order through Nightingale Conant, 1-800-525-9000. Code 786PAS.

How to Gain Power and Influence with People by Tony Alessandra. Six audio cassettes. Order through Nightingale Conant, 1-800-525-9000. Code 370AS.

The Art of Influencing People Positively by Tony Alessandra. 45-minute video. Order through Talico, 1-904-241-1721. Code TI-201.

15. CUSTOMER ORIENTATION

Definition: The ability to demonstrate concern for satisfying one's external and/or internal customers.

An employee demonstrating this competency:

- Quickly and effectively solves customer problems.
- Talks to customers (internal or external) to find out what they want and how satisfied they are with what they are getting.
- Lets customers know he/she is willing to work with them to meet their needs.
- Finds ways to measure and track customer satisfaction.
- Presents a cheerful, positive manner with customers.

Importance of this Competency

Customer Orientation means focusing one's own and the unit's efforts toward meeting the needs of internal and external customers. The principle of customer orientation is at the heart of the total quality movement, which involves continuous improvement to meet and exceed customer requirements. Customer Orientation is also essential for survival in today's increasingly competitive marketplace. Only companies that effectively meet the needs of their customers will survive.

To achieve internal effectiveness and efficiency, organizations must also ensure that individual units are responsive to the needs of their internal customers.

General Considerations in Developing this Competency

This competency requires a particular orientation and attitude, rather than the extensive development of new skills. Thus the primary way to develop this competency is to put it into practice by identifying your unit's internal or external customers, talking to them to understand their needs, and focusing the unit's efforts toward meeting these needs.

Practicing this Competency

Meet with your unit to identify its major customers. List the customers who receive the work outputs from your group. Analyze and prioritize the list. Identify who are your most important customers and who will become your major customers over the next two to three years.

Set up meetings with your key customers. Ask them how satisfied they are with what you are providing them now, and what you can do to provide better service.

With your unit, identify ways to measure the quality and responsiveness of the service you are providing (e.g., number of errors detected in shipments each week and average time from order to delivery).

Create a graph of each key service measure over time, and post the graphs where everyone in your work unit can see them.

Identify and implement improvements in work processes that will result in better customer service.

Obtaining Feedback

Periodically meet with your key customers to review the service you have been providing and identify ways to improve it.

Periodically survey your customers to learn how satisfied they are with your unit's service. Create a survey that includes both quantifiable ratings and open-ended questions.

Identify what work processes or assignments are currently hindering your unit's ability to provide excellent service to its customers. Develop ideas for changing the work processes or assignments and discuss them with your manager.

If your job involves providing direct service to external customers, consider taking a course that provides role plays and feedback on customer interactions.

Learning from Experts

Interview individuals with a reputation for providing excellent service to their customers. Find out what these individuals did to improve their service to their customers.

Coaching Suggestions for Managers

If you are coaching someone who is trying to develop this competency, you can:

- Provide feedback and suggestions to help improve Customer Orientation.
- Demonstrate through your own actions a commitment to providing excellent service.
- Ask this person what you can do to enable him/her to do a better job of focusing on customer service.
- Observe this person in interactions with key internal or external customers and provide specific, constructive feedback.
- Recognize and reward behavior that demonstrates a commitment to customers.

Sample Development Goals

By February 15, I will meet with each of my unit's five key internal customers. I will ask how satisfied they are with the service we are providing and what we can do to improve it.

By March 8, I will meet with Lila Welch to learn what her unit has done to provide excellent service to its internal customers. From this conversation, I will develop a list of specific ideas to consider for application in my unit.

By April 30, I will complete a self-study course in Customer Orientation skills and identify a list of ideas to apply in my own unit.

Books

The Customer-Driven Company by Richard Whitely. Order through Pfeiffer & Co., 1-800-274-4434, Code #GO4AT1.

Delivering Knock-Your-Socks-Off Service by Ron Zemke. Order through Pfeiffer & Co., 1-800-274-4434, Code #H42AT1.

Customer Satisfaction: The Other Half of Your Job by Dru Scott. Order through Crisp Publications. 1-800-442-7477. ISBN 1-56052-084-1.

Customer Focused Quality by Tom Hinton and Wini Schaeffer. Order through American Society for Training and Development, Tel. 703-683-8100. Order Code #HICF.

Self-Study Courses

Keeping Customers for Life. American Management Association Self-Study Course. 1-800-262-9699. Stock #95043CYI.

Managing the Customer Satisfaction Process. American Management Association Self-Study Course. 1-800-262-9699. Stock #94072CYI.

Achieving the Competitive Edge with Customer Service. American Management Association Self-Study Course. 1-800-262-9699. Stock #94050CYI.

Seminars and Workshops

Achieving Excellent Service: An Action Plan for Top Management. Three days. American Management Association Course. Various locations. Tel. 518-891-0065. Mtg. No. 2591T23.

Becoming a Customer-Focused Organization: a series of three workshops. MasteryLab. Tel. 1-800-870-9490.

Business Competencies

16. DIAGNOSTIC INFORMATION GATHERING

Definition: The ability to identify the information needed to clarify a situation, seek that information from appropriate sources, and use skillful questioning to draw out the information when others are reluctant to disclose it.

An employee demonstrating this competency:

- Identifies the specific information needed to clarify a situation or to make a decision.
- Gets more complete and accurate information by checking multiple sources.
- Probes skillfully to get at the facts, when others are reluctant to provide full, detailed information.
- Routinely walks around to see how people are doing and to hear about any problems they are encountering.
- Questions others to assess whether they have thought through a plan of action.
- Questions others to assess their confidence in solving a problem or tackling a situation.
- Asks questions to clarify a situation.
- Seeks the perspective of everyone involved in a situation.
- Seeks out knowledgeable people to obtain information or clarify a problem.

Importance of this Competency

The most important reason to develop this competency is to ensure that you have the right information to make good business decisions. By obtaining the right information, you can discover options to save money and prevent problems. By using this competency, you can also identify potential problems and develop contingency plans to cope with problems.

General Considerations in Developing this Competency

To develop this competency, you need access to technical and other kinds of information relevant to the kinds of decisions and problems you deal with in your work. You should familiarize yourself with the relevant technical publications in your area, identify sources of electronic information, and maintain a network of contacts with people who can provide information and help in your area of work.

Look for opportunities to seek information from multiple sources in order to clarify problems in your work.

Practicing this Competency

If your company maintains a library of technical publications relevant to your area of work, familiarize yourself with its resources so that you will be able to look for the information you may need later on. Consider subscribing to several key technical publications in your area of work. Regularly scan the contents and abstracts of articles for ones relevant to your work.

Find out from other professionals in your field whether bulletin boards or other sources of useful technical information are available on the Internet. If so, you may be able to ask for and receive expert assistance on a timely basis.

Develop and maintain a network of professional contacts who can provide information and assistance when you need it. Remember that these people's willingness to assist you will depend on your ability to be helpful to them; you must be willing to provide help to others as well as seek help from them.

When addressing a problem or task, try asking for the perspective of each person involved.

When you sense that someone may be giving you incomplete information, probe for more information.

When faced with a problem or task, try seeking information from several different sources (e.g., company experts, the Internet, contacts outside of the organization, technical publications).

Obtaining Feedback

Ask your employees, either individually or as a group, what you can do to ensure that you have better information for decision making.

Learning from Experts

Talk to someone who seems to have a wealth of technical or market information. Ask this person what he/she does to obtain that information.

Volunteer for a team or task force headed by someone who is strong in Diagnostic Information Gathering. Note what this person does to gather information on this project.

Coaching Suggestions for Managers

If you are coaching someone who is trying to develop this competency, you can:

- Model this behavior by seeking information from multiple sources and by probing when you sense that the information you are getting is incomplete.
- Have the person team up with someone who is skilled at this competency, on a task that requires information gathering.
- Suggest additional sources of information.

Sample Development Goals

By April 6, I will talk to four contractors on how to proceed with the refrigeration project.

By May 4, I will review the last four years of three key technical publications for articles that may be relevant to the marketing program we are implementing for the western region.

By June 16, I will investigate Internet sources of information relevant to the air distribution problem and identify ideas to bring to the air distribution project team.

Books

Flawless Consulting by Peter Block. Order through Pfeiffer & Co., 1-800-274-4434, Code #245P14.

Is Your Net Working? A Complete Guide to Building Contacts and Career Visibility by Anne Boe and Bettie Young. New York: Wiley, 1989.

Networking: How to Enrich Your Life and Get Things Done by Donald Woods and Shirley Ormerod. Code 03636EB. Order through Pfeiffer & Company, 1-800-274-4434.

Seminars and Workshops

Problem Solving and Decision Making. Three days. American Management Association. Various locations. Tel. 800-262-9699.

EXTEND™ Consulting Skills. Two days. MasteryLab. Tel. 1-800-870-9490.

17. ANALYTICAL THINKING

Definition: The ability to tackle a problem by using a logical, systematic, sequential approach.

An employee demonstrating this competency:

- Makes a systematic comparison of two or more alternatives.
- Notices discrepancies and inconsistencies in available information.
- Identifies a set of features, parameters, or considerations to take into account in analyzing a situation or making a decision.
- Approaches a complex task or problem by breaking it down into its component parts and considering each part in detail.
- Weighs the costs, benefits, risks, and chances for success when making a decision.
- Identifies many possible causes for a problem.
- Carefully weighs the priority of things to be done.

Importance of this Competency

Analytical Thinking provides the basis for most methods and approaches used in problem solving, decision making, project management, time management, and priority setting.

General Considerations in Developing this Competency

This competency is best used by studying and using some analytical method, tool, or process, such as a project management or a database software program. You can also learn Analytical Thinking by working closely with someone who uses an analytical approach to his/her work. This competency is related to Diagnostic Information Gathering.

Practicing this Competency

Read some of the references for this competency and select a problem-solving or decision-making method that you can apply in your own work. Then try it out. Afterwards, ask the group what worked well, what worked less effectively, and what you might do to improve the use of this method.

Take a course in project management and apply what you learn to plan and manage a project.

Use project management software, such as Superproject Expert, Microsoft Project, Time Line, MacProject to plan and manage a project.

Use one of the resources on time management to analyze how you spend your time.

Use a personal organizer system to manage your calendar, to-do list, and personal information. Consider either a paper-based system, such as Day Timers, or a software system, such as ACT! or Lotus Organizer.

When faced with a decision requiring a choice among several alternatives (e.g., which fax machine to buy or which candidate to hire) use a systematic approach, such as this one:

- Identify the criteria to consider in making the decision.
- Establish weights for the criteria.
- Consider and rate each alternative on each of the criteria.
- Develop an overall score for each alternative.

Use a spreadsheet or database program to develop a way to handle some task or problem.

Obtaining Feedback

When you use an analytical approach as the basis for a recommended course of action, ask for feedback from others about how effectively you used this process.

Learning from Experts

Interview someone who has developed a solid analytical process or tool. Ask what the person did to develop the process or tool. Try to get the whole sequence of the person's thoughts and actions. Identify approaches you can apply in your own analytical thinking.

Coaching Suggestions for Managers

If you are coaching someone who is trying to develop this competency, you can:

- Explain any analytical tools and processes you use in your work.
- Provide work assignments that require developing or using an analytical approach.
- Model a systematic thinking process.

Sample Development Goals

By September 20, I will discuss project management software with our MIS group, select a program, study the manual and tutorial materials for it, and apply it to planning and managing the Film Lining Project.

By June 28, I will read *Effective Group Problem Solving* by Fox, and apply the group problem approach described in that book to a problem in my unit.

By July 25, I will interview Bill Meamore about how he uses ECCO Pro software and get a demonstration of this approach.

By August 20, I will develop a detailed project plan for the Eastern Exposition.

Books

Project Management by Marion Haynes. Order through Crisp Publications. 1-800-442-7477. ISBN ISBN0-931961-75-0.

Systematic Problem Solving and Decision Making by Sandy Pokras. Order through Crisp Publications. 1-800-442-7477. ISBN 0-931961-63-7.

Productive Problem Solving by Robert Carkhuff. HRD Press, 1973.

The Art of Problem Solving by Russell Ackoff. Wiley, 1987.

The New Rational Manager by Charles Kepner and Benjamin Tregoe. Kepner-Tregoe, 1981.

Reasoning by Michael Scriven. McGraw-Hill, 1977.

How to Solve It by G. Polya. Princeton University Press, 1971.

Making Tough Decisions. Tactics for Improving Managerial Decision Making by Paul Nutt. Jossey-Bass, 1989.

The Complete Problem Solver: A Total System for Competitive Decision Making by John Arnold. New York: John Wiley & Sons, 1992.

Project Management: How to Plan and Manage Successful Projects by Joan Knutson and Ira Blitz. New York: AMACOM, 1991.

Self-Study Courses

How to be a Successful Project Manager. American Management Association Self-Study Course. 1-800-262-9699. Stock #90079CYI.

Taking Control with Time Management. American Management Association Self-Study Course. 1-800-262-9699. Stock #90038CYI.

The Power of Focused Thinking by Edward de Bono. Audio cassette program. 789PAS, if ordered through Nightingale Conant. 1-800-525-9000.

Seminars and Workshops

Problem Solving and Decision Making. Three days. American Management Association Course. Various locations. Tel. 518-891-0065. Mtg. No. 2504T23.

18. FORWARD THINKING

Definition: The ability to anticipate the implications and consequences of situations and take appropriate action to be prepared for possible contingencies.

An employee who demonstrates this competency:

- Anticipates possible problems and develops contingency plans in advance.
- Notices trends in the industry or marketplace and develops plans to prepare for opportunities or problems.
- Anticipates the consequences of situations and plans accordingly.
- Anticipates how individuals and groups will react to situations and information and plans accordingly.

Importance of this Competency

By using this competency you will be able to notice and take advantage of opportunities, especially ones arising out of trends in the marketplace. You will also be more effective at gaining and maintaining people's support because you will accurately anticipate and be prepared for their reactions to new information and to organizational changes. In a rapidly changing organization and marketplace, Forward Thinking is essential.

General Considerations in Developing this Competency

There are no special skills required to use this competency. Since Forward Thinking requires good information about the people you work with, about your organization, and about your industry and marketplace, you should develop and maintain access to these kinds of information. Maintain a network of contacts who can keep you informed about developments in the organization, industry, and marketplace. Talk regularly to the people with whom you work to understand their interests, concerns, and motivations.

Develop the habit of anticipating what will happen, especially how other individuals will react to situations and information. Make plans based on what you anticipate.

This competency is closely related to two other competencies: Interpersonal Awareness and Diagnostic Information Gathering. Developing those two competencies is likely to help develop Forward Thinking.

Practicing this Competency

Read trade publications and industry journals to identify trends that may affect your company, department, or unit.

Develop and maintain a network of contacts, both inside and outside of your organization, with whom you can discuss developments in your industry and marketplace.

Over a two-week period, take notes on how individuals with whom you work—your boss, your coworkers, the people who report directly to you—react to situations and information. Note patterns for each individual.

When you plan a project, anticipate possible problems that could occur at each step and have a contingency plan ready in case each problem develops. It is often useful to do this with other project team members.

The next time you have potentially surprising or distressing news for someone, try to anticipate how this person will react. Identify what you can do in presenting this information to minimize undesired reactions.

Obtaining Feedback

After managing a project or event, ask others who were involved for feedback about what you could have anticipated and planned for.

Learning from Experts

When you plan a complex project, ask someone strong in Forward Thinking to review the plan with you and to help identify and plan for possible problems.

Volunteer to work on a project team headed by someone strong in forward thinking. Observe what this person does to anticipate and plan for solutions to possible problems.

Coaching Suggestions for Managers

If you are coaching someone who is trying to develop this competency, you can:

- Model forward thinking in your interactions with this person by sharing your own thinking about possible problems and about the likely effect of information and events on others.
- When assigning a project to this person, ask him or her to think of possible problems and plan ways to address these problems.
- Assign this person to a task force or team headed by someone who is strong in Forward Thinking.
- Ask the person to read trade journals or industry publications and to bring ideas about opportunities arising from developments in the marketplace.

Sample Development Goals

By January 17, I will review the project plan for Link Net, identify possible problems or risks associated with each task, and prepare contingency plans to address the problems.

By February 12, I will read the last year's issues of the most important trade journal in my field and make a list of possible opportunities for our organization based on market and industry trends.

By February 29, I will ask the Axle Replacement Team to give me feedback on the degree to which I demonstrated forward thinking in the project plan.

Books

Managing Projects in Organizations by J. D. Frome. San Francisco: Jossey-Bass, 1995.

The Art of Problem Solving by Russell Ackoff. New York: John Wiley & Sons, 1987.

Influence Without Authority by Allan Cohen and David Bradford. New York: John Wiley & Sons, 1991.

Self-Study Courses

Successful Project Management. American Management Association. 800-262-9699. Code #0-7612-0618-3-CGDM.

Seminars and Workshops

Critical Thinking: A New Paradigm for Peak Performance These Days. American Management Association. 800-262-9699.

Problem Solving and Decision Making. Three days. 800-537-6378.

Developing Value-Adding People and Adding Value (for employees). One-Two days each. MasteryLab. Tel. 1-800-870-9490.

19. CONCEPTUAL THINKING

Definition: The ability to find effective solutions by taking a holistic, abstract, or theoretical perspective.

An employee demonstrating this competency:

- Notices similarities between different and apparently unrelated situations.
- Quickly identifies the central or underlying issues in a complex situation.
- Creates a graphic diagram showing a systems view of a situation.
- Develops analogies or metaphors to explain a situation.
- Applies a theoretical framework to understand a specific situation.

Importance of this Competency

Conceptual Thinking underlies the judgment required of managers when they must make decisions in complex situations. Someone with Conceptual Thinking can view a problem from the context of the larger picture of the organization's overall goals and strategy and can put the elements of the problem into proper perspective. Conceptual Thinking is required for solving problems that affect many departments or processes and for problems that require innovative approaches.

General Considerations in Developing this Competency

People who possess this competency have the ability to create an overall understanding of problems or situations by linking information or applying theoretical frameworks. You can strengthen your conceptual thinking abilities by studying and understanding the theoretical concepts that apply to your work. You can learn systems thinking and find ways to apply it on the job.

Practicing this Competency

Attend meetings of professional and trade associations and identify and habitually read trade and professional journals, *The Wall Street Journal*, the business section of your local paper, etc., to gain a wider appreciation for the current business environment and trends in your own business, as well as trends that may affect your customers. Apply what you have learned to solve your own business problems and to provide better customer service.

When confronted with a complex issue, think about whether you have dealt with or heard about similar situations in the past. If so, what is similar? What is different? What worked well in the other situation that would work with your current issue? What didn't work and what can you do to prevent similar problems from occurring in your current situation?

Create graphic diagrams to represent a task or problem.

Take a course in Top Mapping or another systems thinking method and apply what you learn to your own unit or department.

Obtaining Feedback

Discuss your understanding of job-related problems with others who you feel are good at Conceptual Thinking to get their feedback on whether they have come up with the same conclusions as you.

Learning from Experts

Interview someone strong in Conceptual Thinking and ask this person to provide examples of how he/she has applied conceptual thinking in his/her work. Ask for examples of how this person tackled complex problems or decisions.

Attend professional conferences in your technical area to see examples of how others have applied conceptual thinking to problems in your field.

Coaching Suggestions for Managers

If you are coaching someone who is trying to develop this competency, you can:

- Help this person think through a complex problem by considering the problem from the standpoint of issues and changes in the larger organization.
- Provide assignments offering exposure to persons skillful in Conceptual Thinking.
- Provide opportunities such as conferences and courses that will expose this person to others involved with conceptual work.

Sample Development Goals

By December 1, I will read *The Complete Problem Solver* by John Arnold.

By February 1, I will interview Sharon Martrix to see how she conceptualizes issues related to cultural awareness.

Books

The Complete Problem Solver: A Total System for Competitive Decision Making by John D. Arnold. New York: John Wiley and Sons., 1992.

Use Both Sides of Your Brain by Tony Buzan. New York: E.P. Dutton, 1974.

Charting the Corporate Mind: Graphic Solutions to Business Conflicts by Charles Hampden-Turner. New York: McGraw Hill, 1993.

Identifying and Solving Problems: A Systems Approach, 3rd ed., by Roger Kaufman. San Diego: University Associates, 1982.

The New Regional Manager by Charles Kepner and Benjamin Trego. Princeton, New Jersey: Princeton Research Press, 1982.

Analyzing Performance Problems by Robert F. Mager and Peter Pipe. Belmont, California: Fearon, 1970.

Applied Imagination by Alexander Osborne. Charles Scribner's and Sons, 1979.

The Fifth Discipline Fieldbook by Peter Senge, et al. New York: A Currency Book, published by Doubleday, 1994. See Systems Thinking.

The Creative Attitude: Learning to Ask and Answer the Right Questions by Roger Schank and Peter Childers. New York: Macmillan, 1988.

Self-Study Courses

The Benchmaking Course. One multiple choice case study: American Management Association. 1-800-262-9699. Code: #95025R26.

Creative Problem Solving. Four audio cassettes, one workbook, two multiple choice tests. American Management Association. Tel. 1-800-262-9699. Code: #80218CY1.

Systematic Problem Solving and Decision Making by Sandy Pokras. A six-step plan to problem resolution. Self-study exercises, checklists, and case studies. Available from Crisp Publications, Tel. 1-800-442-7477. ISBN 0-931961-63-7.

Seminars and Workshops

Creativity and Innovation: Dynamic Solutions to Work-Related Challenges. Various Locations. American Management Association. Tel. 1-800-262-9699. 2524VQE.

Other Resources

Mind Mapping by Michael Gelb. Four audio cassettes. Order through Nightingale-Conant, 1-800-55-9000. Code 10400AS.

The Innovator: Producing Powerful Ideas. Video tape. The Training Edge. 1-800-292-4375.

Creativity in Business by Carol Kinsey Gorman. Book and accompanying video tape. Available from Crisp Publications. Tel. 1-800-442-7477.

20. STRATEGIC THINKING

Definition: The ability to analyze the organization's competitive position by considering market and industry trends, existing and potential customers (internal and/or external), and strengths and weaknesses as compared to competitors.

An employee demonstrating this competency:

- Understands the organization's strengths and weaknesses as compared to competitors.
- Understands industry and market trends affecting the organization's competitiveness.
- Has an in-depth understanding of competitive products and services within the marketplace.
- Develops and proposes a long-term (3-5 year) strategy for the organization based on an analysis of the industry and marketplace and the organization's current and potential capabilities as compared to competitors.

Importance of this Competency

Strategic Thinking involves analyzing an organization's strengths, weaknesses, and potential in its marketplace and industry and developing a medium-to-long-term plan based on a competitive strategy. This analysis ensures that the organization establishes a direction that will maximize its chances for competitive success. This competency is especially important for senior managers and for middle managers in marketing and sales who are most likely to have interactions with customers and competitors.

General Considerations in Developing this Competency

This competency requires several kinds of knowledge. First, it requires in-depth market and industry knowledge—knowledge of one's own and the competitors' products, processes, customers, and suppliers, and knowledge about trends in the marketplace and industry. You can gain this knowledge by attending industry and trade shows, reading trade and industry publications, and talking with actual and potential customers and industry and market experts.

Second, company knowledge is required. That includes an understanding of the strengths and limitations, both actual and potential, in one's own staff, equipment, resources, and processes. This knowledge enables a company to identify the opportunities it is best positioned to exploit. You can gain company knowledge through company experience and through analysis and evaluation of company processes, staff, and equipment, and other resources.

Another component of this competency is strategic analysis, which is best learned through books and courses.

Strategic Thinking is the product of three other competencies: Diagnostic Information Gathering, Analytical Thinking, and Conceptual Thinking.

Practicing this Competency

Obtain a copy of your company's strategic plan and any related documents. Read the document(s) and identify the implications for your unit. What should your unit be doing to ensure the success of the overall strategic plan?

Attend an industry or trade conference and identify several trends in the industry or marketplace that have implications for your own organization.

Talk to contacts inside or outside your company who have familiarity with your industry and/or marketplace. Ask what they see as trends in the marketplace or industry. Identify possible strategies or action steps that your organization or business unit could take to exploit these trends. Discuss your ideas with your manager, unit, or other appropriate group.

Work on a team that is developing a strategic plan for your organization or unit.

Use a consultant or a self-study guide to help a team from your unit develop a strategic plan.

Use the Internet to gather information about existing and potential customers and about competitors.

Obtaining Feedback

Prepare a strategic analysis of a product line or of your business unit and ask someone whose strategic judgment you respect to review and critique your analysis.

Learning from Experts

Interview someone strong in strategic thinking. Ask what this person does to gain and analyze strategic information.

Coaching Suggestions for Managers

If you are coaching someone who is trying to develop this competency, you can:

- Provide assignments that require Strategic Thinking, such as conducting strategic or market analysis, managing a product line, or developing a strategy for an organizational unit.
- Involve this person in meetings where strategic issues are discussed.

Sample Development Goals

By June 1, I will read Michael Porter's *Competitive Strategy* and prepare a list of ideas that I can apply in my own business unit.

By July 15, I will complete a course on Strategic Planning offered by the American Management Association.

By September 15, I will convene a team to do a strategic analysis and develop a strategic plan for our department.

Books

Strategic Planning Workbook by Karsten Hellebust and Joseph Krallinger. Order through Pfeiffer & Co. 1-800-274-4434. Code #G82AT1.

Choosing the Future by Stuart Wells, Butterworth–Heinemann, 1998. Tel. 800-366-2665.

Strategic Thinking for the Next Economy, Cusumano and Markides, Jossey-Bass, 2001.

Strategic Thinking, Bruce and Langdon, Essential Managers Series, Dorling Kindersley Publishing, 2000.

Self-Study Courses

How to Write a Marketing Plan. American Management Association Self-Study Course. 1-800-262-9699. Stock #94026CYI.

Competitive Strategies: How to Develop Marketing Strategies and Tactics. American Management Association Self Study Course. 1-800-262-9699. Stock #94066CYI.

How to Analyze the Competition. American Management Association Self-Study Course. Tel.: 1-800-262-9699. Stock # 94046CYI.

Strategic Marketing Planning. American Management Association Self-Study Course. 1-800-262-9699. Stock #94054CYI.

How to Develop the Strategic Plan. American Management Association Self-Study Course. 1-800-262-9699. Stock #94035CYI.

Strategic Planning. American Management Association Self-Study Course. 1-800-262-9699. Stock #80190CYI. Includes four audio cassettes.

Seminars and Workshops

Strategic Planning. Three days. American Management Association Course. Various locations. Tel. 518-891-0065. Mtg. No. 2526T23.

Thinking and Managing Strategically. Three days. American Management Association Course. Various locations. Tel. 518-891-0065. Mtg. No. 2530T23.

Applied Strategic Planning. Three days. Offered by UA Consulting & Training Services. Various locations. 619-552-8901. Code: ASP-PC.

Developing the Strategic Leader. Five days. Center for Creative Leadership. Tel. 336-545-2800.

Strategic Management. Five days. NTL Institute. Tel. 800-777-5227.

21. TECHNICAL EXPERTISE

Definition: The ability to demonstrate depth of knowledge and skill in a technical area.

An employee demonstrating this competency:

- Effectively applies technical knowledge to solve a range of problems.
- Possesses an in-depth knowledge and skill in a technical area.
- Develops technical solutions to new or highly complex problems that cannot be solved using existing methods or approaches.
- Is sought out as an expert to provide advice or solutions in his/her technical area.
- Keeps informed about cutting-edge technology in his/her technical area.

Importance of this Competency

A company's technical knowledge and capability is one its most important and often undervalued resources. Senior individual contributors and many managers need Technical Expertise to make decisions and to perform nonstandard technical tasks. As more and more tasks requiring basic technical knowledge become automated, a larger proportion of jobs will require technical problem solving and creativity that depend on Technical Expertise.

General Considerations in Developing this Competency

Technical Expertise requires some technical training and/or education, together with experience that uses that training and knowledge in work processes and methods. Technical Expertise begins with the ability to perform a limited range of technical tasks. With experience, this ability broadens and deepens so that more complex, unusual, and difficult problems can be solved.

Developing this competency requires reading, attending conferences, and taking technical training courses to keep your technical knowledge current. You must also use that knowledge by attempting new and more challenging technical problems.

The three most important ways to develop this competency are self-study, taking courses, and working in partnership with someone more technically skilled than yourself.

Practicing this Competency

Take a technical course that will enhance your technical skills in ways that will benefit the business.

Read professional journals and other technical publications that will keep your skills current.

Volunteer for an assignment that will require you to learn new technical skills.

Look for opportunities to work closely with others from whom you can learn new technical skills.

Attend professional or industry conferences to learn about developments in your technical area.

Volunteer to work on a team developing new technical processes.

Obtain information about new technology, tools, hardware, and software being used in your technical area.

Obtaining Feedback

Prepare a sample of technical work, such as a technical paper, a set of technical recommendations, or a technical tool or process, and ask someone whose technical judgment you respect to critique your work.

Learning from Experts

Look for opportunities to work closely on technical tasks with people from whom you can learn new technical skills.

Coaching Suggestions for Managers

If you are coaching someone who is trying to develop this competency, you can:

- Provide assignments that will develop this person's technical skills.
- Make technical training available.
- Involve this person in meetings where technical issues will be discussed.
- Review and provide feedback on this person's technical work.

Sample Development Goals

By June 1, I will attend one professional conference.

By July 1, I will complete a course in Microsoft Access and plan an application to manage competitive product information.

By November 1, I will join the Extrusion Process Reevaluation Team and attend all meetings.

Books

Consult experts in your area of specialization to identify books, articles, and professional journals to read.

22. INITIATIVE

Definition: Identifying what needs to be done and doing it before being asked or before the situation requires it.

An employee demonstrating this competency:

- Identifies what needs to be done and takes action before being asked or before the situation requires it.
- Does more than what is normally required in a situation.
- Seeks out others involved in a situation to learn their perspectives.
- Takes independent action to change the direction of events.

Importance of this Competency

In many jobs, outstanding performers demonstrate Initiative by seizing opportunities, assuming responsibility, and doing more than what is normally expected in the job. In recent years, job roles have become broader, more flexible, and less dependent on stable job descriptions. More Initiative will also be required as more workers perform their work at home and in the field, away from offices where frequent supervision is possible. Thus Initiative promises to become even more important in the future.

Many other competencies, such as Diagnostic Information Gathering, Managing Change, Fostering Teamwork, Developing Others, Establishing Focus, and Attention to Communication, involve special applications of Initiative.

General Considerations in Developing this Competency

As you map your development strategy for this competency, scan your environment and ask yourself: "What needs to be 'fixed'?" "What needs to be done right away?" "What decisions/actions am I postponing?" "What responsibilities am I avoiding?" "What can I do now to provide great customer service?"

There are some readings and other study materials that can sharpen your understanding of what Initiative is all about. More than skill training, the acquisition of this competency may require an attitude change—a desire to do whatever you can to help the business be successful.

Practicing this Competency

Identify recurring problems for your unit or department and take it upon yourself to develop and implement solutions to these problems. Make a general practice of brainstorming with associates whenever you feel stuck or blocked in moving ahead with an idea or solving a problem. Take action to change something that is not in the best interests of the business. Don't wait for deadlines to find out that the work someone was doing for you isn't done. Touch base with the person periodically before the deadline to find out how he or she is doing. If the person is having trouble, help him or her figure out how to solve the problem and still meet the deadline. Join a team or task force where you will have to solve organizational problems with a short deadline.

Obtaining Feedback

Ask your manager, coworkers, and teammates for feedback on your performance after you have completed a project in which you have taken leadership or played a major role. Ask for specific examples of what you did that moved the work along and find out ways in which you could have been more effective. Ask what you could be doing to take more initiative in the future.

Learning from Experts

Talk to someone who has demonstrated a high level of initiative. Ask this person to talk about several times when he/she demonstrated significant initiative. Find out what the person did and how. Ask what problems the person encountered and how he/she dealt with them.

Coaching Suggestions for Managers

If you are coaching someone who is trying to develop this competency, you can:

- Empower the individual by giving the person projects where he or she has the responsibility for working out the details after you have outlined the goals and requirements.
- Expect the person to take ownership of his or her work and responsibility for the results. Acknowledge and praise the person for behavior that demonstrates Initiative.
- Clarify the areas where any Initiative is welcome and the areas where it is important to get support for ideas before moving ahead.

Sample Development Goals

By January 18, I will develop a one-page summary sheet for sales reps, comparing Hart Company's X65 valve with our YJ911.

On the next annual department report, due on February 6, I will provide a table of contents to make it easier for readers to locate the information they need.

I will volunteer for the Network Reengineering Team and serve on it from June through December.

Books

Flight of the Buffalo by James A. Belasco and Ralph C. Strayer. New York: Warner Books, 1993. Strayer. New York: Warner Books, 1993.

Doing it Now by Edwin C. Bliss. New York: Bantam, 1984.

Getting Things Done by Edwin C. Bliss. New York: Macmillian, 1991.

The Seven Habits of Highly Effective People by Stephen Covey. New York: Simon & Schuster, 1990. See especially Habit 1: Be Proactive.

The Creative Attitude by Roger Shank and Peter Childers. New York: Macmillan, 1988.

Self-Study Courses

Self -Empowerment: How to take Charge of your Work Life. Three audio cassettes, plus a workbook and two self-tests; American Management Association. 1-800-262-9699. Code 80182R26.

Stop Procrastinating: Go to Work! A book with exercises and worksheets to help you get to work and be more productive. Crisp Publications. 1-800-262-9699. ISBN 0-931061-88-2.

Seminars and Workshops

Assertiveness Training for Managers. American Management Association. 1-800-262-9699. Various Locations. 25273DC.

Intuitive Leadership: Turning Gut Feelings into Competitive Advantage. American Management Association. 1-800-262-9699. Various Locations. 277VQE.

Developing Value-Adding People and Adding Value (for employees). One-Two days each. MasteryLab. Tel. 1-800-870-9490.

Other Resources

The Seven Habits of Highly Effective People by Stephen Covey. Six audio cassettes. Order through Nightingale Conant, 1-800-525-9000. Code 786PAS.

The Shape of the Winner by Tom Peters. Video tape. Coronet/MTI Film and Video. 1-800-621-2131.

People and Productivity: We Learn from the Japanese. Video tape. The Training Edge. 1-800-292-4375.

23. ENTREPRENEURIAL ORIENTATION

Definition: The ability to look for and seize profitable business opportunities; willingness to take calculated risks to achieve business goals.

An employee demonstrating this competency:

- Notices and seizes profitable business opportunities.
- Stays abreast of business, industry and market information that may reveal business opportunities.
- Demonstrates willingness to take calculated risks to achieve business goals.
- Proposes innovative business deals to potential customers, suppliers, and business partners.
- Encourages and supports entrepreneurial behavior in others.

Importance of this Competency

Entrepreneurial Orientation, looking for and seizing profitable business opportunities, has always been a central determinant of success in business and in sales. As companies decentralize, setting up separate business units, more business leaders must develop Entrepreneurial Orientation. The variety of new business deals and the speed with which they are arranged add to the importance of this competency.

General Considerations in Developing this Competency

Entrepreneurial Orientation requires some business knowledge. You must know the kinds of business deals that are possible and their associated legal and financial arrangements. These kinds of knowledge can be gained through reading business publications, taking courses, and talking with others who have these kinds of business knowledge.

But this competency also requires a particular set of attitudes: alertness to opportunities and comfort with calculated risk taking. Working with people skilled in this competency is an excellent way to develop these attitudes.

Practicing this Competency

Read business publications such as *Business Week, Fortune, The Wall Street Journal* and other relevant industry and trade journals to learn about the types of business deals that are available in your industry.

Identify and interview someone in your industry who is skilled in Entrepreneurial Orientation. Ask what this person does to become aware of and seize business opportunities. Ask the person to talk about what he/she did to put together several business deals.

Develop and maintain a network of contacts in your industry or marketplace—people from whom you may be able to learn about business opportunities.

Ask customers and suppliers for referrals, i.e., others who may be interested in doing business with you.

Identify possible opportunities and discuss them with others who may be able to help you act on these opportunities.

Encourage reasonable risk taking in the people who work for you. Do not expect every opportunity to pay off. If you criticize or punish people for taking reasonable risks, they will avoid this behavior in the future.

Analyze an opportunity using a systematic approach. What are all the foreseeable risks? How likely is each risk? What is the possible payoff under various conditions? How likely is the payoff under those conditions? How can you structure a deal to maximize potential payoff, while minimizing risk?

Obtaining Feedback

When you have identified and analyzed an opportunity, review your analysis with someone whose judgment you trust.

Learning from Experts

Look for opportunities to work closely with someone who has a track record of making successful business deals.

Interview someone who has made several successful business deals. Find out what the person did and how, problems that were encountered, and what the person did to cope with them.

Coaching Suggestions for Managers

If you are coaching someone who is trying to develop this competency, you can:

- Provide assignments that involve working with others who are looking for or putting together business deals.
- Discuss the kinds of business opportunities that the person might pursue.

Sample Development Goals

By December 8, I will identify and prepare an analysis of a potential business deal and review this analysis with Sam Smith and Molly Boult.

By November 20, I will talk to twelve business contacts about the kinds of business opportunities my unit could pursue.

Books

Intrapreneuring by Gifford Pinchot. New York: Harper and Row, 1985.

Seminars and Workshops

Corporate Entrepreneurship. Three days. Institute of Entrepreneurship and Executive Education. Tel. 800-672-7223, Ext. 5092.

24. FOSTERING INNOVATION

Definition: The ability to develop, sponsor or support the introduction of new and improved methods, products, procedures, or technologies.

An employee demonstrating this competency:

- Personally develops a new product or service.
- Personally develops a new method or approach.
- Sponsors the development of new products, services, methods, or procedures.
- Proposes new approaches, methods, or technologies.
- Develops better, faster, or less expensive ways to do things.
- Works cooperatively with others to produce innovative solutions.

Importance of this Competency

Successfully implementing this competency leads to new and improved products and services and new, more effective work processes and procedures that enable quantum leaps in productivity and profitability. The increased competitiveness of the workplace places a premium on this competency; companies that do not innovate will not survive. The total quality movement, by embracing continuous improvement, is based on this competency, as is reengineering—the process of reviewing and totally reconstructing work processes. Rapid developments in information technology also create pressures and opportunities for innovation.

General Considerations in Developing this Competency

At an individual level, this competency requires creativity and commitment to quality. Individuals can develop this competency by learning about creative problem-solving methods and by honing their technical skills. But significant innovation also requires organizational support. The organization must provide incentives, rewards, structures, and training to promote innovation. This requires leaders who value innovation and have the organizational savvy to implement the changes necessary to support it. Promoting and implementing innovation requires communication and influence skills, which are addressed under the competencies Persuasive Communication and Influencing Others.

Practicing this Competency

Volunteer to work on a team attempting to improve a product, process, or service. Then work with the team to generate ideas for improvement, select and refine the ideas, and implement them.

Read a book to identify a technique for problem solving or creative thinking. Apply the technique in your own work or with a team.

Develop and implement an improvement in a product, service, or work process in your work unit.

Obtaining Feedback

If you are a manager, ask the people who work for you what you can do to help foster innovation, both within the unit and through cooperation with other groups.

Learning from Experts

Interview someone who successfully developed or sponsored the development of a significant innovation. Consider people both within and outside of your organization. Ask for a detailed account of what the person did and how. Make a list of ideas that you can implement yourself.

Coaching Suggestions for Managers

If you are coaching someone who is trying to develop this competency, you can:

- Provide opportunities for training in areas such as problem solving and change management.
- Provide opportunities for training in technical skills needed for innovation in a particular area.
- Assign the person to teams involved in developing innovations or in implementing change.
- Recognize and reward innovative behavior.

Sample Development Goals

By May 3, I will complete the AMA self study course in creative problem solving and prepare a list of ideas that I can apply in my own work.

During the spring, I will volunteer to serve on an improvement team and contribute actively.

By July 14, I will form a team to identify and implement improvements in our commercialization process.

Books

Innovation by Thomas Kuczmarski, NTC Business Books and the American Marketing Association, 1995.

Positive Turbulence by Stanley Gruskiewicz, Center for Creative Leadership and Jossey-Bass, 1999.

When Sparks Fly by Dorothy Leonard and Walter Swap, Harvard Business School Press, 1999.

Continuous Improvement and Measurement for Total Quality by Dennis Kinlaw. Order through Pfeiffer & Co., 1-800-274-4434, Code #770AT1.

Developing Products in Half the Time by Preston Smith and Donald Reinertsen. Order through Association for Quality and Participation, 1-513-381-1959. VN02H.

Self-Study Courses

How to Qualify for ISO 9000. American Management Association Self-Study Course. 1-800-262-9699. Stock #95003CYI.

The Benchmarking Course. American Management Association Self-Study Course. 1-800-262-9699. Stock #95025CYI.

Total Quality Management. American Management Association Self-Study Course. 1-800-262-9699. Stock #95025CYI.

Creating a Competitive Advantage Through Innovation. American Management Association Self-Study Course. 1-800-262-9699. Stock #94090CYI.

Creative Problem Solving. American Management Association Self-Study Course. 1-800-262-9699. Stock #80218CYI. Includes four audio cassettes.

Seminars and Workshops

Corporate Innovation. Three days. Institute of Entrepreneurship and Executive Education. Tel. 800-672-7223, Ext. 5092.

25. RESULTS ORIENTATION

Definition: The ability to focus on the desired result of one's own or one's units work; setting challenging goals, focusing effort on the goals, and meeting or exceeding them.

An employee demonstrating this competency:

- Develops challenging but achievable goals.
- Develops clear goals for meetings and projects.
- Maintains commitment to goals in the face of obstacles and frustrations.
- Finds or creates ways to measure performance against goals.
- Exerts unusual effort over time to achieve a goal.
- Has a strong sense of urgency about solving problems and getting work done.

Importance of this Competency

Results Orientation enables an individual to set and achieve challenging goals. People with this competency keep their goals and performance measures firmly in mind, so that they accomplish more in a shorter period of time. This competency is also an advantage after downsizing, because staff of a leaner organization must accomplish more work and become more productive.

General Considerations in Developing this Competency

One of the best ways to develop this competency is to work closely with a manager or team leader who demonstrates it. These people set challenging but achievable goals and milestones and regularly check their progress against goals. They also demonstrate a sense of urgency about achieving goals. You may also find it helpful to try one of the readings or self-study courses that addresses goal setting. In addition to the ideas below, examine the time management readings and courses listed under Analytical Thinking.

Practicing this Competency

Prepare a set of personal work-related goals for the next two weeks. List what you will do in specific terms.

The next time you are in charge of a meeting, prepare an agenda that includes specific objectives. Keep the group on track to ensure that you meet all objectives for the meeting.

Find ways to measure your own work or a team's work. First identify the most important outcomes you are working toward with each key task. Develop a way to measure each key outcome. For example, if you are in a sales group, you might measure number of cold calls, number of customer meetings, number of proposals, and number of sales closed per week. Once you have identified the measures, graph each measure to track trends over time. One such graph might plot number of customer meetings held per week.

If you are on a team, push the team to identify specific goals with deadlines and specific team members accountable for their completion.

Obtaining Feedback

Prepare a set of goals for your own work or for a team of which you are a part. Show the goals to someone whose judgment you respect. Ask if the goals represent the right balance between being challenging and being achievable. A good set of goals should be challenging enough to provide positive motivation and realistic enough to be achievable with some extra effort.

Learning from Experts

Interview someone who has achieved impressive results. Ask this person what he/she does to achieve results. Ask the person to describe in detail what he/she did to achieve one or two impressive results. Ask about planning, setting goals, and dealing with obstacles.

Coaching Suggestions for Managers

If you are coaching someone who is trying to develop this competency, you can:

- Model this competency by publicly setting challenging but achievable goals for your unit.
- Ask the person to prepare a set of personal work-related goals for the next 3–6 months. Review the goals with this person and provide feedback and suggestions. Set up a procedure for the person to regularly meet with you or keep you informed about progress toward the goals.
- Provide assignments that involve having the person work closely with someone who is strong in Results Orientation.

Sample Development Goals

By January 16, I will prepare a set of personal work-related goals for the first quarter and review these goals with my manager.

By February 1, I will develop 3–6 key measures of my work progress. I will plot each of these measures on a graph displayed in my cubicle.

By March 4, I will ensure that the Distribution Reassessment Team has developed a set of goals for the second quarter and an action plan with specific tasks, milestones, and accountabilities. By June 30, the team will meet all of its goals.

Books

Goals and Goal Setting by Larrie Rouillard. Order through Crisp Publications. 1-800-442-7477. ISBN 1-50652-183-X.

Performance Management by Aubrey Daniels. Tucker, Georgia: Performance Management Publications, 1989. 1-404-493-5080.

The Seven Habits of Highly Effective People by Stephen Covey. New York: Simon and Schuster, 1989. Especially Habit 2: Begin with End in Mind.

Seminars and Workshops

Managing Performance—With Competence. (Adding Value through PM). Three days each. MasteryLab. Tel. 1-800-870-9490.

Other Resources

The Seven Habits of Highly Effective People by Stephen Covey. Six audio cassettes. Order through Nightingale Conant, 1-800-525-9000. Code 786PAS.

26. THOROUGHNESS

Definition: Ensuring that one's own and others' work and information are complete and accurate; carefully preparing for meetings and presentations; following up with others to ensure that agreements and commitments have been fulfilled.

An employee demonstrating this competency:

- Sets up procedures to ensure high quality of work (e.g., review meetings).
- Monitors the quality of work.
- Verifies information.
- Checks the accuracy of own and others' work.
- Develops and uses systems to organize and keep track of information or work progress.
- Carefully prepares for meetings and presentations.
- Organizes information or materials for others.
- Carefully reviews and checks the accuracy of information in work reports (e.g., production, sales, financial performance) provided by management, management information systems, or other individuals and groups.

Importance of this Competency

Thoroughness involves careful preparation, completeness of execution, careful checking of work, and follow-up with others, to ensure that work is on track. Thoroughness is often undervalued, but it is a competency possessed by most good managers and all good project managers.

Reflect on your own work experience. What problems have you experienced because of lack of thoroughness? You can probably think of a number of situations where more thoroughness would have prevented problems.

General Considerations in Developing this Competency

Developing this competency is largely a matter of disciplining yourself to plan carefully, to check work carefully for errors, and to follow up with others to ensure that they have done what they promised to do. These behaviors are not difficult to learn, but they may be difficult to apply, especially if they conflict with your personal style.

Project management is a method with procedures and systems to ensure Thoroughness. If you are in charge of projects involving many activities and several people, books and courses on project management may be helpful.

Time management systems may also be helpful, especially systems that help you manage your to-do lists and follow-up activities.

Practicing this Competency

For the next meeting or presentation where you will play a key role, take time for careful planning. Think about what you will say or present and what materials you will want to bring. After the meeting, think about how the planning helped you. What problems were avoided?

Before submitting a report or mailing a letter or memo, read it carefully and count the number of errors you discover and correct.

Use a time management system (either a paper-based one or one of the personal information management software programs) with a "tickler" system that allows you to set dates for follow-up actions (e.g., call John on May 20 to see if his part of the presentation is done) and prompts you to perform the follow-up action on the date set.

Ask someone else to review a memo or report and provide feedback and suggestions before you send it out.

Take a course on project management and apply the approach to your next work project.

Obtaining Feedback

Ask your manager or a coworker to observe you and review your work over a one-week period and let you know when your Thoroughness slips.

Show a coworker the behaviors for Thoroughness and ask this person to suggest specific things you could do to improve your Thoroughness.

Learning from Experts

Talk to someone skilled in Thoroughness to find out what this person does to achieve it.

Coaching Suggestions for Managers

If you are coaching someone who is trying to develop this competency, you can:

- Stress the importance of Thoroughness.
- Model thoroughness in your own behavior.
- Ask the person to check his/her work carefully before submitting it.
- Carefully review the person's work and provide feedback on all problems due to lack of Thoroughness.
- Praise the person for work that demonstrates Thoroughness.
- Provide opportunities for the person to learn project management.

Sample Development Goals

By April 20, I will identify and carefully plan for a meeting at which I expect to play a key role.

By April 1, I will talk to all of my immediate coworkers and ask them to let me know whenever they see typographical or other errors in my work.

By May 8, I will complete the AMA self-study course on project management and apply the approach to planning an individual or team project.

Books

Project Management by Marion Haynes. Order through Crisp Publications.
1-800-442-7477. ISBN ISBN0-931961-75-0.

Project Management: How to Plan and Manage Successful Projects by Joan Knutson and
Ira Blitz. New York: AMACOM, 1991.

Self-Study Courses

How to be a Successful Project Manager. American Management Association Self-
Study Course. 1-800-262-9699. Stock #90079CYI.

Taking Control with Time Management. American Management Association Self-
Study Course. 1-800-262-9699. Stock #90038CYI.

27. DECISIVENESS

Definition: The ability to make difficult decisions in a timely manner.

An employee demonstrating this competency:

- Is willing to make decisions in difficult or ambiguous situations, when time is critical.
- Takes charge of a group when it is necessary to facilitate change, overcome an impasse, face issues, or ensure that decisions are made.
- Makes tough decisions (e.g., closing a facility, reducing staff, accepting or rejecting a high-stakes deal).

Importance of this Competency

Leaders, especially those in senior management, need to be decisive. They must be able to make high-stakes decisions, such as whether to accept a multimillion dollar deal, restructure the organization, cancel a venture that is not going well, shut down a plant, or eliminate a large number of jobs. Decisiveness does not mean making decisions impulsively or intuitively; it does mean willingness to step up to a decision when a decision is needed.

General Considerations in Developing this Competency

One of the best ways to learn this competency is to be thrust into a situation in which time-critical decisions are required that compel you to make the best decisions you can under pressure. It may also help to work closely with a leader who demonstrates decisiveness, to see first hand how this person makes decisions.

Another approach is to reflect on your own behavior. Think of situations in which you needed to make a decision. What did you do? Did you act decisively? Would you handle this situation the same way today? What would you do differently?

Practicing this Competency

Volunteer for assignments in which you will be responsible for making decisions.
Practice using a simple analytical process in making decisions by answering these questions:

- What are the criteria that should be considered in making this decision?
- What are the alternatives?
- For each alternative:

    What are the positive results if things go well?
    Can you quantify the benefits of a positive outcome?
    What are the possible risks? What could go wrong?
    Can you quantify the costs of a negative outcome?
    What is the probability of a positive outcome?

Look for opportunities to take charge of a group to overcome an impasse, ensure that the group faces an issue, or change the direction in which the group is moving.

Obtaining Feedback

Ask someone to observe you over a one-month period and give you feedback regarding Decisiveness. Ask this person to point out when you are demonstrating Decisiveness effectively, when you are making decisions too hastily, and when you need to be more decisive.

Learning from Experts

If you have the opportunity to work closely with a decisive leader, observe this person's decision-making behavior. How does this person make decisions?

Interview a leader who is skilled in Decisiveness. Ask the person to talk about several situations in which he/she had to make a decision. Ask the person to walk you through each situation. Find out what the person did, said, and thought in the process of making each decision. Reflect on what you have heard. What behaviors could you benefit from by adopting them?

Coaching Suggestions for Managers

If you are coaching someone who is trying to develop this competency, you can:

- Give the person ongoing, constructive feedback about behavior in decision-making situations.
- Empower this person to make decisions in his/her area of work.
- Provide assignments that involve decision making.
- Be supportive when a decision does not work out. Decisive people do not always make decisions that work out as planned. Rather than criticize the employee, debrief the situation with the employee to help identify what can be learned from it.

Sample Development Goals

By December 1, I will interview Mary Byrne to learn how she makes decisions.

At the next meeting of the Production Team, I will intervene quickly if the group starts to go off track. Afterwards, I will ask two team members for feedback on my behavior.

On March 1, I will review the proposals from different vendors and make a decision on that day.

Within one week, I will confront Deborah about her performance problem and begin implementing the disciplinary process.

Books

The Leadership Factor by John Kotter. New York: Free Press, 1988.

Leadership: What Effective Managers Really Do and How They Do It by Leonard Sayles. New York: McGraw-Hill, 1989.

Making Tough Decisions: Tactics for Improving Managerial Decision Making by Paul Nutt. San Francisco: Jossey-Bass, 1989.

Productive Problem Solving by Robert Carkhuff. Amherst, MA: Human Resource Development Press, 1973.

Seminars and Workshops

Problem Solving and Decision Making. Three days. American Management Association Course. Various locations. Tel. 518-891-0065. Mtg. No. 2504T23.

Self-Management Competencies

28. SELF CONFIDENCE

Definition: Faith in one's own ideas and capability to be successful; willingness to take an independent position in the face of opposition.

An employee demonstrating this competency:

• Is confident of own ability to accomplish goals.
• Presents self crisply and impressively.
• Is willing to speak up to the right person or group at the right time, when he/she disagrees with a decision or strategy.
• Approaches challenging tasks with a "can-do" attitude.

Importance of this Competency

Self confidence is both an attitude about yourself and a quality that others infer based on your behavior and style. If you feel confident about your judgment and ability, you may do things like volunteer for challenging tasks, take risks, and challenge others. These are behaviors that often result in success. Whether others believe you have self confidence depends both on these behaviors and on your general style of behavior. If you are generally upbeat and poised, others will believe you are confident, and they may also believe that you are likely to be successful, in which case they will support your ideas, provide opportunities, and follow when you attempt to provide leadership.

General Considerations in Developing this Competency

Confidence in your ability to be successful is in part an expectation based on past experience. The more successes you have had, the more likely you are to develop faith in your ability to be successful in the future. You can build this kind of confidence by setting and attaining moderately challenging goals.

The confidence that you project to others depends on how comfortable you appear in interpersonal interactions, especially when you are speaking, presenting, or leading a group. You can build this kind of confidence through repeated experience with these kinds of interactions.

Practicing this Competency

Set goals that are moderately challenging—tasks that are within your capability based on past experience, but which require you to extend your capabilities and skills to some degree.

When tackling a challenging task, think of similar tasks that you have successfully managed in the past. Think of the people you can call on if you find that you need help. Act on what you can do to maximize chances for success.

Speak up when you disagree with a decision or approach. State your concerns and the reasons for them, and suggest an alternative approach. Be sure to do this early on, when people may be willing to modify the decision or approach.

In stressful situations, try to project calmness and a sense of being in control.

Obtaining Feedback

Ask someone to observe you speaking to a group or at a meeting. Ask this person to note what you are doing that helps and hinders projecting self confidence.

Learning from Experts

Observe someone who seems to project self confidence. Note what the person says and does that creates this effect.

Coaching Suggestions for Managers

If you are coaching someone who is trying to develop this competency, you can:

- Model a confident manner yourself.
- Provide assignments that the person should be able to complete successfully. Gradually increase the difficulty of the assignments, but avoid making them so difficult that the person is likely to fail.
- Provide the resources, information, and training needed to ensure this person's success.
- Recognize and reward the person for significant accomplishments.
- Observe this person in group interactions. Provide feedback on what the person does that builds or interferes with an impression of confidence.
- Thank the person for speaking up when he/she disagrees with you.

Sample Development Goals

By December 15, I will complete a self-study course in assertiveness.
At the meeting with Brewster's team, on January 12, I will have Judy observe as I try to project self confidence. Afterwards, I will get her feedback and suggestions.

By January 5, I will read Sonya Hamlin's book *How to Talk So People Listen,* and prepare a list of ideas to apply at my next sales presentation.

Books

How to Talk So People Listen by Sonya Hamlin. Order through Association for Quality and Participation, 1-513-381-2959. HR06P.

The Quick and Easy Way to Effective Speaking by Dale and Dorothy Carnegie. New York: The Associated Press Pocket Books, 1977.

Self-Study Courses

Getting Assertive. American Management Association Self-Study Course. 1-800-262-9699. Stock # 92013CYI.

Self-Empowerment: How to Take Charge of Your Work Life. American Management Association Self-Study Course. 1-800-262-9699. Stock #80182CYI. Includes three audio cassettes.

Seminars and Workshops

Toastmasters offers courses designed to increase your confidence in public speaking.

Irresistable You! One day. MasteryLab. Tel. 1-800-870-9490.

Developing Value-Adding People and Adding Value (for employees). One-Two days each. MasteryLab. Tel. 1-800-870-9490.

29. STRESS MANAGEMENT

Definition: The ability to keep functioning effectively when under pressure and maintain self control in the face of hostility or provocation.

An employee demonstrating this competency:

• Remains calm under stress.
• Can effectively handle several problems or tasks at once.
• Controls his/her response when criticized, attacked or provoked.
• Maintains a sense of humor under difficult circumstances.
• Manages own behavior to prevent or reduce feelings of stress.

Importance of this Competency

Stress Management is an essential competency in any job that involves high levels of stress because of a need to meet continual deadlines, to make decisions under pressure, or to deal frequently with upset and angry people.

In recent years many more jobs involve high levels of stress because of increased pressure for results, threats of job loss, and an organizational environment involving continual change. Thus stress management is becoming more important for many more people.

General Considerations in Developing this Competency

To develop this competency, there are a variety of steps you can take to condition your body to better handle stress. First, it is critically important to maintain a balance between your work and the rest of your life by allowing yourself time to enjoy leisure activities and time with family and friends. Regular exercise several times a week is also beneficial. If you have been feeling unusually stressed, a program to learn and practice regular meditation may be helpful.

In addition to these general life-style changes, there are some specific job-related skills (e.g., time management and dealing with upset people) that you can develop through books or courses.

Practicing this Competency

Practice remaining calm in stressful situations. Try to project a sense that you are calm and in control of the situation.

Use a personal information management system (either a paper-based system such as Day Timers or a software program such as ACT! or Lotus Organizer) to manage multiple projects. Learn to use the tickler or alarm system to remind you of upcoming meetings and deadlines.

Begin a program of regular exercise, such as walking or jogging during the lunch hour.

Read *The Relaxation Response* by Herbert Benson, and try regularly meditating every day.

Encourage coworkers to practice stress management activities.

Find and implement ways to make work tasks more fun.

Obtaining Feedback

Ask a coworker to observe you over a one-week period and tell you when you are exhibiting signs of stress.

Ask coworkers to tell you what behaviors you exhibit that either manifest or transmit stress and what behaviors you exhibit that reflect good control of stress.

Learning from Experts

Talk to someone who is effective in managing stress. Ask what this person does to prevent stress and what he/she does to cope with highly stressful situations. Ask for descriptions of how the person handled specific, stressful situations.

Coaching Suggestions for Managers

If you are coaching someone who is trying to develop this competency, you can:

- Model effective stress management.
- Make yourself available as a resource to discuss how to manage stressful situations.

Sample Development Goals

By April 19, I will interview Joe Stourdy and ask him how he manages stress.

By May 20, I will complete a stress management course and begin applying what I have learned.

By June 15, I will read *Coping with Difficult People* by Robert Bramson, and begin applying what I have learned in my interactions with Yma Weiner.

Books

Controlling Stress in the Workplace by Rex Gatto. Order through Pfeiffer & Co., 1-800-274-4434, Code #42184AT1.

Managing Stress for Mental Fitness by Merill Raber & George Dyck. Order through Crisp Publications. 1-800-442-7477. ISBN 1-56052-200-3.

The Time Trap: The New Version of the 20 Year Classic by Alec Mackenzie. AMACOM, 1991.

A Strategy for Handling Executive Stress by Ari Kiev. Nelson-Hall, 1971.

The Relaxation Response by Herbert Benson. Random House Value, 1992.

Stress Without Distress by H. Selye. NAL-Dutton, 1975.

How to Get Control of Your Time and Your Life by Alan Lakein. McKay, 1975.

Coping with Difficult People by Robert Bramson. N.Y.: Ballantine Books, 1981.

Working with Emotional Intelligence by Daniel Coleman. New York: Bantam Books, 1998. See especially Chapter 5, "Self Control."

Self-Study Courses

Personal Strategies for Managing Stress. American Management Association Self-Study Course. 1-800-262-9699. Stock #94012CYI.

Seminars and Workshops

Consult local community college, hospital, and adult education offerings for courses on stress management and meditation.

30. PERSONAL CREDIBILITY

Definition: Demonstrated concern that one be perceived as responsible, reliable, and trustworthy.

An employee demonstrating this competency:

• Does what he/she commits to doing.
• Respects the confidentiality of information or concerns shared by others.
• Is honest and forthright with people.
• Carries his/her fair share of the workload.
• Takes responsibility for own mistakes; does not blame others.
• Conveys a command of the relevant facts and information.

Importance of this Competency

Personal Credibility involves other people's perceptions of three personal characteristics: reliability, trustworthiness, and competence. Reliability means fulfilling promises and commitments. If you consistently demonstrate reliability, other people will assign important responsibilities and leadership roles to you. If you are trustworthy, others will share their real concerns and feelings with you, and you will be able to use this information to influence them by finding win-win solutions. If others perceive you as competent in your technical area, they will seek your services. Your overall credibility determines whether others will treat you as a serious player in your organization.

Someone who lacks credibility is likely to be left out of key decisions and not considered for important positions. Without credibility, it is difficult to enlist others' support and cooperation.

General Considerations in Developing this Competency

Since Personal Credibility is based on others' perceptions, the only way to develop this competency is to alter those perceptions by demonstrating a track record of reliability, trustworthiness, and competence. You can enhance your credibility by taking steps to ensure the visibility of your accomplishments, by making presentations, and by distributing reports and recommendations. But be sure to give credit to everyone else who helped or assisted you in your efforts.

Keep in mind that people have long memories for actions and events that reflect negatively on credibility. If you fail to fulfill a commitment or betray a confidence, you will lose credibility with the persons involved, and it will take significant effort on your part to repair the damage.

Practicing this Competency

Volunteer for tasks and make sure that you fulfill commitments on time with high quality work.

Volunteer for leadership roles.

Volunteer for assignments that will provide exposure and allow you to demonstrate credibility to higher management and to people in other parts of the organization.

When others share personal information or perceptions of coworkers, assume that this information is confidential and do not disclose it to others.

Never lie to people. If you are unable or unwilling to disclose something, say so and explain why.

As a team member, be sure to carry a fair share of the workload.

Accept responsibility for your mistakes; avoid blaming others.

When preparing a recommendation, make sure you have obtained the relevant facts and information.

Prepare thoroughly for presentations.

Seek advice or help from appropriate experts to avoid presenting recommendations that reflect your own lack of knowledge.

Obtaining Feedback

Let coworkers know that you are working to enhance your Personal Credibility. Show them the definition and behaviors for this competency. Ask them to observe you over a one-month period and let you know when you do something that either detracts from or enhances your credibility.

Learning from Experts

Observe someone who has a high level of Personal Credibility. Look for evidence of the behaviors associated with this competency. Note what the person does that seems to enhance his/her credibility.

Coaching Suggestions for Managers

If you are coaching someone who is trying to develop this competency, you can:

- Model this competency in your own personal interactions by fulfilling promises, demonstrating honesty, and respecting confidences.
- Make sure that the person has realistic but challenging goals and the information and resources needed to achieve these goals.
- Encourage this person to volunteer for assignments or responsibilities that will build this person's credibility with others, especially higher management and people in other parts of the organization.
- Keep informed about this person's progress against his/her goals and commitments, so that if there is a danger of not meeting a commitment, you can help this person find a way to meet the commitment.

Sample Development Goals

By March 15, I will volunteer for three assignments on the Unit Planning Team.
By April 16, I will prepare and give a presentation on the results of our benchmarking activities with Tri-Plex and King Systems.

By May 10, I will read *Credibility* by Kouzes and Posner, and prepare a list of ideas I can apply in my role as Team Leader of the Sales Expansion Team.

Books

Credibility: How Leaders Gain and Lose It, Why People Demand It by James Kouzes and Barry Posner. Order through Pfeiffer & Co., 1-800-274-4434, Code #J10C34.

Ethics in Business: A Guide for Managers by Robert Maddux and Dorothy Maddux. Order through Crisp Publications. 1-800-442-7477. ISBN 0-931961-69-6.

The Seven Habits of Highly Effective People by Stephen Covey. Code D2108. Order through HRD Discount Book Society, 215-292-2650.

Principle-Centered Leadership by Stephen Covey. Code D902. Order through HRD Discount Book Society, 215-292-2650.

Tough Choices: Managers Talk Ethics. New York: Wiley, 1986.

Seminars and Workshops

Leadership Impact Lab. Three days plus follow-up. Institute of Entrepreneurship and Executive Education. Tel. 800-672-7223, Ext. 5092.

The Competent Leader. Three days. MasteryLab. Tel. 1-800-870-9490.

Developing Value-Adding People and Adding Value (for employees). One-Two days each. MasteryLab. Tel. 1-800-870-9490.

31. FLEXIBILITY

Definition: Being open to different and new ways of doing things; willingness to modify one's preferred way of doing things.

An employee demonstrating this competency:

- Is able to see the merits of perspectives other than his/her own.
- Demonstrates openness to new organizational structures, procedures, and technology.
- Switches to a different strategy when an initially selected one is unsuccessful.
- Demonstrates willingness to modify a strongly held position in the face of contrary evidence.

Importance of this Competency

People who can work with a wide variety of people and find mutually acceptable solutions have always been in demand. In recent years, organizations have undergone sweeping changes, and the ability to adapt to change has become an essential requirement. The redesign of work processes and roles and the introduction of information technology have led to broader and ever-changing job responsibilities. People who cannot demonstrate flexibility will not survive in most organizations.

Flexibility does not mean being agreeable to whatever others want to do. Outstanding performers are results-oriented and maintain firm commitment to their goals. They are flexible regarding methods to achieve the goals, and they enlist others' support for the goals.

General Considerations in Developing this Competency

To develop Flexibility, you should learn to understand and appreciate perspectives other than your own. This means listening to others and genuinely trying to understand their concerns and feelings. It also means thinking about issues from the perspective of what is best for the overall organization, given its strategy and plans.

Developing this competency also means demonstrating openness to change (e.g., by actively learning and supporting a new work process or information technology). Change is difficult because it requires setting aside methods that are comfortable and replacing them with new methods that are at first uncomfortable to use. You must be willing to persist through the initial period of discomfort to achieve comfort and enhanced effectiveness with the new methods.

Practicing this Competency

When you discover that you disagree with someone regarding a policy, decision, or project, ask this person to explain his/her perspective. Listen, periodically paraphrasing what you hear, but do not express disagreement. Allow the person to fully explain his/her perspective. Comment on what you like and can support in this person's position.

Volunteer for assignments that involve working with internal and external groups that are new to you.

Take a leadership role in supporting the implementation of new technology or work processes.

Obtaining Feedback

Let coworkers know that you are working to develop this competency. Ask them to observe you over a one-month period and to let you know when you demonstrate Flexibility or a lack of Flexibility.

Learning from Experts

Observe someone with a reputation for Flexibility over a period of one month. Note what this person does when faced with obstacles and changing circumstances.

Interview someone who has adapted effectively to change. Ask what strategies and approaches this person used to adapt to organizational changes.

Coaching Suggestions for Managers

If you are coaching someone who is trying to develop this competency, you can:

- Model openness to change in your own behavior.
- Provide assignments that require dealing with new work processes or technology or working with different internal or external groups.
- Notice and praise behaviors reflecting Flexibility.
- Let this person know when he/she is demonstrating behavior that does not indicate Flexibility.

Sample Development Goals

By May 5, I will set up a luncheon meeting with Gary Vynes (a team member in the Training Department who seems to have a different perspective than mine on the kind of training we should be providing for first-line supervisors). I will ask him to explain his perspective on training first-line supervisors. I will listen, summarize, ask questions to clarify, and identify parts of his views that I can support.

By May 10, I will learn to use our new presentation software and apply it in a presentation to the Relocation Team.

Books

Adapting to Change: Making it Work for You by Carol Goman. Order through Crisp Publications. 1-800-442-7477. ISBN 1-56052-192-9.

Seminars and Workshops

Developing Value-Adding People and Adding Value (for employees). One-Two days each. MasteryLab. Tel. 1-800-870-9490.

Core Competencies

The following is a summarized list of the 31 competencies discussed in the book, listed by "cluster" (similar competencies related to a common skill set). Each competency includes a definition and the observable behaviors that may indicate the existence of a competency in a person.

COMPETENCIES DEALING WITH PEOPLE

The Leading Others Cluster

1. Establishing Focus

Definition: The ability to develop and communicate goals in support of the business' mission.

- Acts to align own unit's goals with the strategic direction of the business.
- Ensures that people in the unit understand how their work relates to the business' mission.
- Ensures that everyone understands and identifies with the unit's mission.
- Ensures that the unit develops goals and a plan to help fulfill the business' mission.

2. Providing Motivational Support

Definition: The ability to enhance others' commitment to their work.

- Recognizes and rewards people for their achievements.
- Acknowledges and thanks people for their contributions.
- Expresses pride in the group and encourages people to feel good about their accomplishments.
- Finds creative ways to make people's work rewarding.
- Signals own commitment to a process by being personally present and involved at key events.

- Identifies and promptly tackles morale problems.
- Gives talks or presentations that energize groups.

3. Fostering Teamwork

Definition: As a team member, the ability and desire to work cooperatively with others on a team; as a team leader, the ability to demonstrate interest, skill, and success in getting groups to learn to work together.

Behaviors for Team Members

- Listens and responds constructively to other team members' ideas.
- Offers support for others' ideas and proposals.
- Is open with other team members about his/her concerns.
- Expresses disagreement constructively (e.g., by emphasizing points of agreement, suggesting alternatives that may be acceptable to the group).
- Reinforces team members for their contributions.
- Gives honest and constructive feedback to other team members.
- Provides assistance to others when they need it.
- Works for solutions that all team members can support.
- Shares his/her expertise with others.
- Seeks opportunities to work on teams as a means to develop experience and knowledge.
- Provides assistance, information, or other support to others, to build or maintain relationships with them.

Behaviors for Team Leaders

- Provides opportunities for people to learn to work together as a team.
- Enlists the active participation of everyone.
- Promotes cooperation with other work units.
- Ensures that all team members are treated fairly.
- Recognizes and encourages the behaviors that contribute to teamwork.

4. Empowering Others

Definition: The ability to convey confidence in employees' ability to be successful, especially at challenging new tasks; delegating significant responsibility and authority; allowing employees freedom to decide how they will accomplish their goals and resolve issues.

- Gives people latitude to make decisions in their own sphere of work.
- Is able to let others make decisions and take charge.
- Encourages individuals and groups to set their own goals, consistent with business goals.
- Expresses confidence in the ability of others to be successful.
- Encourages groups to resolve problems on their own; avoids prescribing a solution.

5. Managing Change

Definition: The ability to demonstrate support for innovation and for organizational changes needed to improve the organization's effectiveness; initiating, sponsoring, and implementing organizational change; helping others to successfully manage organizational change.

Employee Behaviors

- Personally develops a new method or approach.
- Proposes new approaches, methods, or technologies.
- Develops better, faster, or less expensive ways to do things.

Manager/Leader Behaviors

- Works cooperatively with others to produce innovative solutions.
- Takes the lead in setting new business directions, partnerships, policies or procedures.
- Seizes opportunities to influence the future direction of an organizational unit or the overall business.
- Helps employees to develop a clear understanding of what they will need to do differently, as a result of changes in the organization.
- Implements or supports various change management activities (e.g., communications, education, team development, coaching).
- Establishes structures and processes to plan and manage the orderly implementation of change.
- Helps individuals and groups manage the anxiety associated with significant change.
- Facilitates groups or teams through the problem-solving and creative-thinking processes leading to the development and implementation of new approaches, systems, structures, and methods.

6. Developing Others

Definition: The ability to delegate responsibility and to work with others and coach them to develop their capabilities.

- Provides helpful, behaviorally specific feedback to others.
- Shares information, advice, and suggestions to help others to be more successful; provides effective coaching.
- Gives people assignments that will help develop their abilities.
- Regularly meets with employees to review their development progress.
- Recognizes and reinforces people's developmental efforts and improvements.
- Expresses confidence in others' ability to be successful.

7. Managing Performance

Definition: The ability to take responsibility for one's own or one's employees' performance, by setting clear goals and expectations, tracking progress against the goals, ensuring feedback, and addressing performance problems and issues promptly.

Behaviors for employees

- With his/her manager, sets specific, measurable goals that are realistic but challenging, with dates for accomplishment.
- With his/her manager, clarifies expectations about what will be done and how.
- Enlists his/her manager's support in obtaining the information, resources, and training needed to accomplish his/her work effectively.
- Promptly notifies his/her manager about any problems that affect his/her ability to accomplish planned goals.
- Seeks performance feedback from his/her manager and from others with whom he/she interacts on the job.
- Prepares a personal development plan with specific goals and a timeline for their accomplishment.
- Takes significant action to develop skills needed for effectiveness in current or future job.

Behaviors for managers

- Ensures that employees have clear goals and responsibilities.
- Works with employees to set and communicate performance standards that are specific and measurable.
- Supports employees in their efforts to achieve job goals (e.g., by providing resources, removing obstacles, acting as a buffer).
- Stays informed about employees' progress and performance through both formal methods (e.g., status reports) and informal methods (e.g., management by walking around).
- Provides specific performance feedback, both positive and corrective, as soon as possible after an event.
- Deals firmly and promptly with performance problems; lets people know what is expected of them and when.

Communication and Influencing Cluster

8. Attention to Communication

Definition: The ability to ensure that information is passed on to others who should be kept informed.

- Ensures that others involved in a project or effort are kept informed about developments and plans.
- Ensures that important information from his/her management is shared with his/her employees and others as appropriate.
- Shares ideas and information with others who might find them useful.
- Uses multiple channels or means to communicate important messages (e.g., memos, newsletters, meetings, electronic mail).
- Keeps his/her manager informed about progress and problems; avoids surprises.
- Ensures that regular, consistent communication takes place.

9. Oral Communication

Definition: The ability to express oneself clearly in conversations and interactions with others.

- Speaks clearly and can be easily understood.
- Tailors the content of speech to the level and experience of the audience.
- Uses appropriate grammar and choice of words in oral speech.
- Organizes ideas clearly in oral speech.
- Expresses ideas concisely in oral speech.
- Maintains eye contact when speaking with others.
- Summarizes or paraphrases his/her understanding of what others have said to verify understanding and prevent miscommunication.

10. Written Communication

Definition: The ability to express oneself clearly in business writing.

- Expresses ideas clearly and concisely in writing.
- Organizes written ideas clearly and signals the organization to the reader (e.g., through an introductory paragraph or through use of headings).
- Tailors written communications to effectively reach an audience.
- Uses graphics and other aids to clarify complex or technical information.
- Spells correctly.
- Writes using concrete, specific language.
- Uses punctuation correctly.
- Writes grammatically.
- Uses an appropriate business writing style.

11. Persuasive Communication

Definition: The ability to plan and deliver oral and written communications that make an impact and persuade their intended audiences.

- Identifies and presents information or data that will have a strong effect on others.
- Selects language and examples tailored to the level and experience of the audience.
- Selects stories, analogies, or examples to illustrate a point.
- Creates graphics, overheads, or slides that display information clearly and with high impact.
- Presents several different arguments in support of a position.

12. Interpersonal Awareness

Definition: The ability to notice, interpret, and anticipate others' concerns and feelings, and to communicate this awareness empathetically to others.

- Understands the interests and important concerns of others.
- Notices and accurately interprets what others are feeling, based on their choice of words, tone of voice, expressions, and other nonverbal behavior.
- Anticipates how others will react to a situation.

- Listens attentively to people's ideas and concerns.
- Understands both the strengths and weaknesses of others.
- Understands the unspoken meaning in a situation.
- Says or does things to address others' concerns.
- Finds non-threatening ways to approach others about sensitive issues.
- Makes others feel comfortable by responding in ways that convey interest in what they have to say.

13. Influencing Others

Definition: The ability to gain others' support for ideas, proposals, projects, and solutions.

- Presents arguments that address others' most important concerns and issues and looks for win-win solutions.
- Involves others in a process or decision to ensure their support.
- Offers trade-offs or exchanges to gain commitment.
- Identifies and proposes solutions that benefit all parties involved in a situation.
- Enlists experts or third parties to influence others.
- Develops other indirect strategies to influence others.
- Knows when to escalate critical issues to own or others' management, if own efforts to enlist support have not succeeded.
- Structures situations (e.g., the setting, persons present, sequence of events) to create a desired impact and to maximize the chances of a favorable outcome.
- Works to make a particular impression on others.
- Identifies and targets influence efforts at the real decision makers and those who can influence them.
- Seeks out and builds relationships with others who can provide information, intelligence, career support, potential business, and other forms of help.
- Takes a personal interest in others (e.g., by asking about their concerns, interests, family, friends, hobbies) to develop relationships.
- Accurately anticipates the implications of events or decisions for various stakeholders in the organization and plans strategy accordingly.

14. Building Collaborative Relationships

Definition: The ability to develop, maintain, and strengthen partnerships with others inside or outside the organization who can provide information, assistance, and support.

- Asks about the other person's personal experiences, interests, and family.
- Asks questions to identify shared interest, experiences, or other common ground.
- Shows an interest in what others have to say; acknowledges their perspectives and ideas.
- Recognizes the business concerns and perspectives of others.
- Expresses gratitude and appreciation to others who have provided information, assistance, or support.
- Takes time to get to know coworkers, to build rapport and establish a common bond.
- Tries to build relationships with people whose assistance, cooperation, and support may be needed.
- Provides assistance, information, and support to others to build a basis for future reciprocity.

15. Customer Orientation

Definition: The ability to demonstrate concern for satisfying one's external and/or internal customers.

- Quickly and effectively solves customer problems.
- Talks to customers (internal or external) to find out what they want and how satisfied they are with what they are getting.
- Lets customers know he/she is willing to work with them to meet their needs.
- Finds ways to measure and track customer satisfaction.
- Presents a cheerful, positive manner with customers.

COMPETENCIES DEALING WITH BUSINESS

The Preventing and Solving Problems Cluster

16. Diagnostic Information Gathering

Definition: The ability to identify the information needed to clarify a situation, seek that information from appropriate sources, and use skillful questioning to draw out the information, when others are reluctant to disclose it

- Identifies the specific information needed to clarify a situation or to make a decision.
- Gets more complete and accurate information by checking multiple sources.
- Probes skillfully to get at the facts, when others are reluctant to provide full, detailed information.
- Routinely walks around to see how people are doing and to hear about any problems they are encountering.
- Questions others to assess whether they have thought through a plan of action.
- Questions others to assess their confidence in solving a problem or tackling a situation.
- Asks questions to clarify a situation.
- Seeks the perspective of everyone involved in a situation.
- Seeks out knowledgeable people to obtain information or clarify a problem.

17. Analytical Thinking

Definition: The ability to tackle a problem by using a logical, systematic, sequential approach.

- Makes a systematic comparison of two or more alternatives.
- Notices discrepancies and inconsistencies in available information.
- Identifies a set of features, parameters, or considerations to take into account, in analyzing a situation or making a decision.
- Approaches a complex task or problem by breaking it down into its component parts and considering each part in detail.
- Weighs the costs, benefits, risks, and chances for success, in making a decision.
- Identifies many possible causes for a problem.
- Carefully weighs the priority of things to be done.

18. Forward Thinking

Definition: The ability to anticipate the implications and consequences of situations and take appropriate action to be prepared for possible contingencies.

- Anticipates possible problems and develops contingency plans in advance.
- Notices trends in the industry or marketplace and develops plans to prepare for opportunities or problems.
- Anticipates the consequences of situations and plans accordingly.
- Anticipates how individuals and groups will react to situations and information and plans accordingly.

19. Conceptual Thinking

Definition: The ability to find effective solutions by taking a holistic, abstract, or theoretical perspective.

- Notices similarities between different and apparently unrelated situations.
- Quickly identifies the central or underlying issues in a complex situation.
- Creates a graphic diagram showing a systems view of a situation.
- Develops analogies or metaphors to explain a situation.
- Applies a theoretical framework to understand a specific situation.

20. Strategic Thinking

Definition: The ability to analyze the organization's competitive position by considering market and industry trends, existing and potential customers (internal and external), and strengths and weaknesses as compared to competitors.

- Understands the organization's strengths and weaknesses as compared to competitors.
- Understands industry and market trends affecting the organization's competitiveness.
- Has an in-depth understanding of competitive products and services within the marketplace.
- Develops and proposes a long-term (3–5 year) strategy for the organization based on an analysis of the industry and marketplace and the organization's current and potential capabilities as compared to competitors.

21. Technical Expertise

Definition: The ability to demonstrate depth of knowledge and skill in a technical area.

- Effectively applies technical knowledge to solve a range of problems.
- Possesses an in-depth knowledge and skill in a technical area.
- Develops technical solutions to new or highly complex problems that cannot be solved using existing methods or approaches.
- Is sought out as an expert to provide advice or solutions in his/her technical area.
- Keeps informed about cutting-edge technology in his/her technical area.

The Achieving Results Cluster

22. Initiative

Definition: Identifying what needs to be done and doing it before being asked or before the situation requires it.

- Identifying what needs to be done and takes action before being asked or the situation requires it.
- Does more than what is normally required in a situation.
- Seeks out others involved in a situation to learn their perspectives.
- Takes independent action to change the direction of events.

23. Entrepreneurial Orientation

Definition: The ability to look for and seize profitable business opportunities; willingness to take calculated risks to achieve business goals.

- Notices and seizes profitable business opportunities.
- Stays abreast of business, industry, and market information that may reveal business opportunities.
- Demonstrates willingness to take calculated risks to achieve business goals.
- Proposes innovative business deals to potential customers, suppliers, and business partners.
- Encourages and supports entrepreneurial behavior in others.

24. Fostering Innovation

Definition: The ability to develop, sponsor, or support the introduction of new and improved method, products, procedures, or technologies.

- Personally develops a new product or service.
- Personally develops a new method or approach.
- Sponsors the development of new products, services, methods, or procedures.
- Proposes new approaches, methods, or technologies.
- Develops better, faster, or less expensive ways to do things.
- Works cooperatively with others to produce innovative solutions.

25. Results Orientation

Definition: The ability to focus on the desired result of one's own or one's unit's work, setting challenging goals, focusing effort on the goals, and meeting or exceeding them.

- Develops challenging but achievable goals.
- Develops clear goals for meetings and projects.
- Maintains commitment to goals in the face of obstacles and frustrations.
- Finds or creates ways to measure performance against goals.

- Exerts unusual effort over time to achieve a goal.
- Has a strong sense of urgency about solving problems and getting work done.

26. Thoroughness

Definition: Ensuring that one's own and others' work and information are complete and accurate; carefully preparing for meetings and presentations; following up with others to ensure that agreements and commitments have been fulfilled.

- Sets up procedures to ensure high quality of work (e.g., review meetings).
- Monitors the quality of work.
- Verifies information.
- Checks the accuracy of own and others' work.
- Develops and uses systems to organize and keep track of information or work progress.
- Carefully prepares for meetings and presentations.
- Organizes information or materials for others.
- Carefully reviews and checks the accuracy of information in work reports (e.g., production, sales, financial performance) provided by management, management information systems, or other individuals and groups.

27. Decisiveness

Definition: The ability to make difficult decisions in a timely manner.

- Is willing to make decisions in difficult or ambiguous situations, when time is critical.
- Takes charge of a group when it is necessary to facilitate change, overcome an impasse, face issues, or ensure that decisions are made.
- Makes tough decisions (e.g., closing a facility, reducing staff, accepting or rejecting a high-stakes deal).

SELF-MANAGEMENT COMPETENCIES

28. Self Confidence

Definition: Faith in one's own ideas and capability to be successful; willingness to take an independent position in the face of opposition.

- Is confident of own ability to accomplish goals.
- Presents self crisply and impressively.
- Is willing to speak up to the right person or group at the right time, when he/she disagrees with a decision or strategy.
- Approaches challenging tasks with a "can-do" attitude.

29. Stress Management

Definition: The ability to keep functioning effectively when under pressure and maintain self control in the face of hostility or provocation.

- Remains calm under stress.
- Can effectively handle several problems or tasks at once.
- Controls his/her response when criticized, attacked or provoked.
- Maintains a sense of humor under difficult circumstances.
- Manages own behavior to prevent or reduce feelings of stress.

30. Personal Credibility

Definition: Demonstrated concern that one be perceived as responsible, reliable, and trustworthy.

- Does what he/she commits to doing.
- Respects the confidentiality of information or concerns shared by others.
- Is honest and forthright with people.
- Carries his/her fair share of the workload.
- Takes responsibility for own mistakes; does not blame others.
- Conveys a command of the relevant facts and information.

31. Flexibility

Definition: Openness to different and new ways of doing things; willingness to modify one's preferred way of doing things.

- Is able to see the merits of perspectives other than his/her own.
- Demonstrates openness to new organizational structures, procedures, and technology.
- Switches to a different strategy when an initially selected one is unsuccessful.
- Demonstrates willingness to modify a strongly held position in the face of contrary evidence.

Worksheets for Career Planning and Self-Assessment

The following are the worksheets used throughout the book that you may want to use to aid in your career assessment and planning.

My transferable competencies dealing with

PEOPLE

I AM GOOD AT

Leading Others

Establishing Focus
Developing and communicating goals in support of the business' mission

H M L

Providing Motivational Support
Enhancing others' commitment to their work

H M L

Fostering Teamwork
Getting groups to learn to work together cooperatively

H M L

Empowering Others
Conveying confidence in employees' ability to be successful, allowing employees freedom to decide how they will accomplish their goals and resolve issues

H M L

Managing Change
Initiating, sponsoring, or championing organizational change; helping others to successfully manage organizational change

H M L

Developing Others
Delegating responsibility and coaching others to develop their capabilities

H M L

Managing Performance
Taking responsibility for one's own or one's employees' performance by setting clear goals and expectations

H M L

Communicating And Influencing

Attention To Communication
Ensuring that information is passed on to others who should be kept informed

H M L

Oral Communication
Expressing oneself clearly in conversations and interactions with others

H M L

Written Communication
Expressing oneself clearly in business writing

H M L

Persuasive Communication
Planning and delivering oral and written communications that persuade intended audiences

H M L

Interpersonal Awareness
Noticing, interpreting and anticipating others' concerns and feelings, and communicating this awareness empathetically to others

H M L

Influence Skill
Gaining others' support for ideas, proposals, projects, and solutions

H M L

Building Collaborative Relationships
Developing and maintaining partnerships with others

H M L

Customer Orientation
Demonstrating concern for satisfying one's external and/or internal customers

H M L

My transferable competencies dealing with

BUSINESS

I AM GOOD AT

Preventing And Solving Problems

Diagnostic Information Gathering
Identifying the information needed to
clarify a situation, seeking that information
from appropriate sources, and using skillful
questioning to draw out the information

H M L

Analytical Thinking
Approaching a problem by using a logical,
systematic, sequential approach

H M L

Forward Thinking
Anticipating the implications and consequences
of situations and taking appropriate action
to be prepared for possible contingencies

H M L

Conceptual Thinking
Finding effective solutions by taking a holistic,
abstract or theoretical perspective

H M L

Strategic Thinking
Analyzing your competitive position by considering
market and industry trends, existing and
potential customers, and strengths and
weaknesses as compared to competitors

H M L

Technical Expertise
Depth of knowledge and skill in a technical area

H M L

Achieving Results

Initiative
Identifying what needs to be done
and doing it before being asked
or before the situation requires it

H **M** L

Entrepreneurial Orientation
Looking for and seizing profitable business
opportunities; taking calculated risks
to achieve business goals

H M L

Fostering Innovation
Demonstrating support for innovation and
for organizational changes needed
to improve the organization's effectiveness

H M L

Results Orientation
Focusing on the desired result of one's
own or one's unit's work; setting challenging
goals, focusing effort on the goals, and
meeting or exceeding them

H M L

Thoroughness
Ensuring that one's own and others' work and
information are complete and accurate; careful
preparation for meetings and presentations;
following up with others to ensure that agreements
and commitments have been fulfilled

H M L

Decisiveness
Making difficult decisions
in a timely manner

H M L

My transferable competencies dealing with

SELF MANAGEMENT

I AM GOOD AT

Self Confidence
Faith in one's own ideas and ability to be
successful; taking an independent position
in the face of opposition

H M L

Stress Management
Functioning effectively when under pressure
and maintaining self control in
the face of hostility or provocation

H M L

Personal Credibility
Demonstrating concern that one be perceived
as responsible, reliable, and trustworthy

H M L

Flexibility
Openness to different and new ways
of doing things; willingness to modify one's
preferred way of doing things

H M L

IDENTIFYING YOUR STRONGEST COMPETENCIES

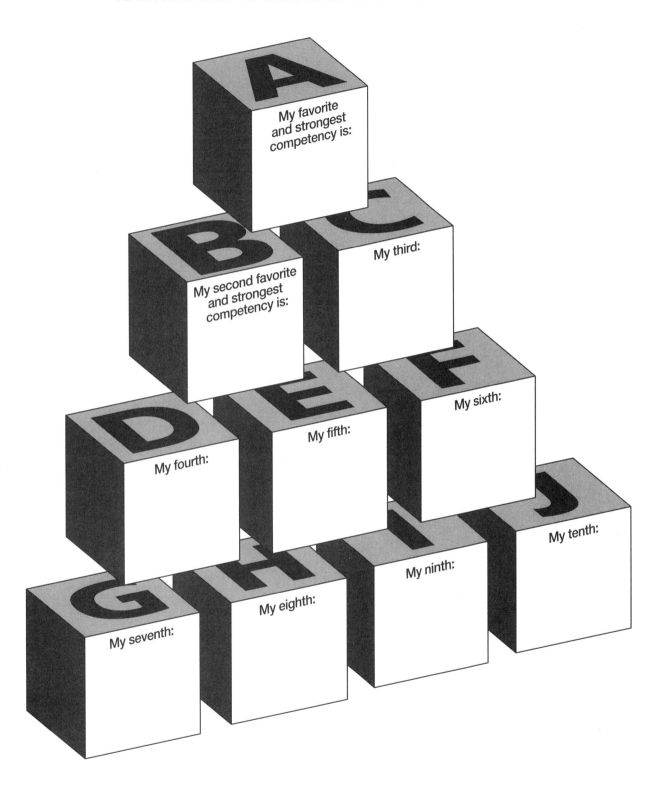

CAREER PLANNING DIAGRAM

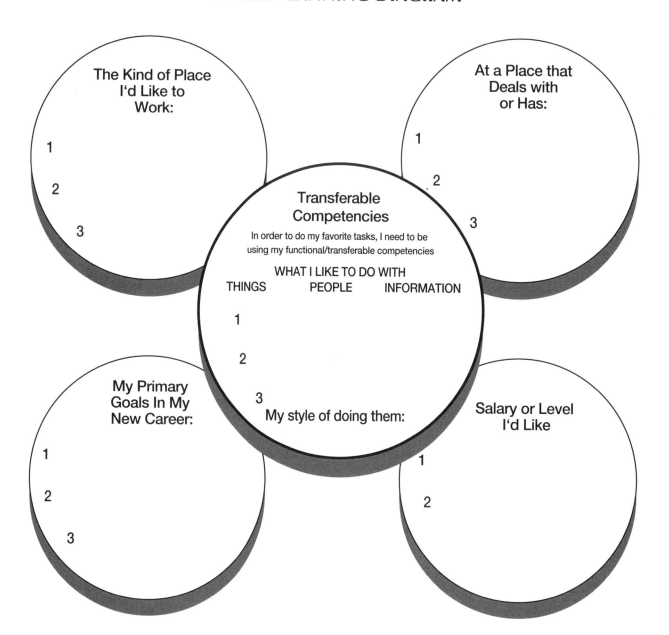

COMPETENCY SELECTOR

Employee: _____ Date: _____

Instructions: If there are competencies identified for your job, check these competencies in column A. Read the definition and behaviors for each competency (Appendix A). Then check any boxes that apply in columns B–G. After completing this process for all thirty-one competencies, use column G to select three competencies to target for your personal development.

	A	B	C	D	E	F	G
	IDENTIFIED FOR MY JOB	IMPROVE PERFORMANCE OF RESPONSIBILITIES I MOST NEED TO IMPROVE	SUPPORTS MY KEY JOB GOALS FOR NEXT 6 MONTHS	NEEDED FOR CAREER ADVANCEMENT	SELF ASSESSMENT IS LOW	SUPERVISOR'S OR OTHERS' ASSESSMENT IS LOW	SELECTED TO DEVELOP
1 Establishing Focus							
2 Providing Motivational Support							
3 Fostering Teamwork							
4 Empowering Others							
5 Managing Change							
6 Developing Others							
7 Managing Performance							
8 Attention to Communication							
9 Oral Communication							
10 Written Communication							
11 Persuasive Communication							
12 Interpersonal Awareness							
13 Influencing Others							
14 Building Collaborative Relationships							
15 Customer Orientation							
16 Diagnostic Information Gathering							
17 Analytical Thinking							
18 Forward Thinking							
19 Conceptual Thinking							
20 Strategic Thinking							
21 Technical Expertise							
22 Initiative							
23 Entrepreneurial Orientation							
24 Fostering Innovation							
25 Results Orientation							
26 Thoroughness							
27 Decisiveness							
28 Self Confidence							
29 Stress Management							
30 Personal Credibility							
31 Flexibility							

Consolidated Development Plan

COMPETENCY DEVELOPMENT PLANNING FORM

Employee: _____ Manager: _____ Date: _____

Competency Targeted for Development: _____

Reasons: _____

Specify the 3–4 month period when you will work on this competency: _____

COMPETENCY DEVELOPMENT GOALS	TARGETED COMPLETION DATE	ACTUAL COMPLETION DATE

Signatures:

Employee: _____ Manager: _____

Consolidated Development Plan

CAPITALIZING ON YOUR STRENGTHS

Decide which three competencies represent your greatest strengths and decide how you can build on those strengths to enhance your effectiveness.

For each strength set one goal. Break down each goal into specific and measurable activities. Indicate the involvement of others that will be required. Commit to accomplishing the activities by a specific completion date.

Step 1: Strength	Step 2: Specific Activities	Step 3: Involvement of Others	Step 4: Completion date
Strength: Goal:			
Strength: Goal:			
Strength: Goal:			

Consolidated Development Plan

MEETING YOUR DEVELOPMENT NEEDS

Choose three competencies you really want to improve.

Again, for each development need set one goal. Then, break down each goal into specific and measurable activities. Indicate the involvement of others that will be required. Finally, commit to accomplishing the activities by a specific completion date.

Step 1: Development Need	Step 2: Specific Activities	Step 3: Involvement of Others	Step 4: Completion date
Development Need: Goal:			
Development Need: Goal:			
Development Need: Goal:			

Example of a Job Competency Model

A Job Model for a Division Executive Team

Why show this model as an example rather than a more "typical" job?

For those of you who aspire to higher levels of responsibility, this model may provide some insight into the performance and competency requirements of many executive level positions. This can be another source of information when you complete column A of the Competency Selector worksheet.

Keep in mind that, although this model contains elements common to most executive staff positions, it is not a generic model. An executive staff position in your organization may differ in some very key areas. It is best to seek the advice of an executive in your own organization, or start with the counsel of your immediate supervisor or the human resources department.

Introduction

This job model includes:

- a summary of the main responsibilities.
- a detailed description of the main responsibilities, showing key tasks and performance outcomes/measures.
- the core competencies identified as most important for effectiveness in this job, with descriptions of specific behaviors contributing to effectiveness.

The selected set of core competencies provides a focus for performance management and development for people in the job. The selected set does not include all the skills and competencies that are important in this job.

Summary of Main Responsibilities

1. Responsibility for the financial performance of the business
2. Managing change for organizational improvement

3. Management of a function (Including managing a cost base)
4. Planning: both medium term (1-2 years) and long-term strategic
5. Performance management
6. Communicating upward and downward
7. Satisfying external and internal customers
8. Ensuring compliance with the law

Detailed Description of Main Responsibilities

1. Responsibility for the Financial Performance of the Business

Main Tasks

- Establishing a budget
- Controlling costs
- Exceeding the budget
- Achieving sales goals
- Achieving growth
- Achieving income goals
- Recommending and justifying investment

Performance Outcomes and Measures

- Income targets
- Return on capital employed
- Cost control numbers
- Rate of growth of the business

2. Managing Change for Organizational Improvement

Main Tasks

- Identifying opportunities for improvement
- Leading the process of redesigning structures, systems, and processes by which work is accomplished
- Sponsoring and championing experimentation with new approaches
- Educating people about the need for organizational change and about what the changes will mean for them

Performance Outcomes and Measures

- Specific, detailed plans for organizational change within the function
- Implementation of organizational changes within the function
- Improvements in quantitative performance measures (e.g., reduced costs, waste, cycle time; increased productivity, sales) due to organizational improvements
- Employee understanding of and support for organizational change

3. Management of a Function (Including Managing a Cost Base)

Main Tasks

- Preparing a budget
- Identifying tasks within the function
- Setting goals, targets, and objectives
- Anticipating, responding to, and managing change
- Establishing measurements of performance
- Staffing with the right people
- Organizing the function
- Communicating within and across the function

Performance Outcomes and Measures

- Meeting goals and targets—both financial and non-financial
- Continuous improvement
- Function's goals align with the business
- Provision of opportunities for people
- Satisfaction and morale of employees
- Reputation of the function

4. Planning: Both Medium-Term (1–2 years) and Long-Term Strategic

Main Tasks

- Preparing growth plans
- Preparing financial plans
- Preparing capital allocation plans
- Identifying an overall strategic thrust
- Assessing the market, competition, customers, technology, labor force, and suppliers; scanning the environment
- Identify what we are good at—our advantage
- Identify how to match resources with objectives
- Identify short-term options
- Understand whether the strategy and goals are aligned with the corporation's goals

Performance Outcomes and Measures

- Goals are met
- Articulated strategy and plan
- Management is not surprised
- Always ahead of the competition
- Proactive instead of reactive

5. Performance Management

Main Tasks

- Assessing employees' potential
- Identifying and providing opportunities for development
- Assessing employees' strengths and deficiencies
- Coaching
- Providing honest feedback on performance
- Delegating
- Removing non-performers

Performance Outcomes and Measures

- A pool of people to select from for next jobs
- Direct reports are promoted
- Executive staff person is promoted
- Unit's reputation is enhanced (its people are sought out)
- Fewer performance issues

6. Communicating Upward and Downward: Strategy, Resources and Performance Against Objectives

Main Tasks

- Communicating downward: policy, procedures, direction, and the spirit of the business
- Understanding the big picture and strategy
- Establishing lines of communication—through employees
- Understanding how one's own organization fits in
- Stating broad policies and procedures for consistency, but not so narrowly as to inhibit
- Monitoring compliance: ensuring that policies and procedures are understood
- Selling what one is communicating
- Developing policies and procedures that work
- Communicating frequently
- Getting people to change the way they do things
- Communicating upward: strategy, resources needed, and performance against objectives
- Identifying what would be well received by upper management
- Holding one-to-one sessions with upper management
- Giving presentations to upper management
- Simplifying complex information so that it can be easily understood by senior management
- Putting the message in terms that senior management can relate to
- Educating senior management about the business

Performance Outcomes and Measures

- A focused organization
- More satisfied employees
- Everyone understands the direction and where they fit
- Better, quicker decisions made at lower levels
- An empowered workforce
- Achievement and maintenance of ISO certification
- Unit is more likely to achieve its goals
- Unit obtains the resources needed to accomplish its goals

7. Satisfying External and Internal Customers

Main Tasks

- Finding out what customers want
- Getting feedback directly
- Interpreting indirect feedback
- Instilling customer service attitudes in employees
- Translating customer requirements into our terminology
- Identifying who our customers are, especially the ones we don't interact with directly
- Soliciting feedback from customers
- Reaching agreement with customers about what satisfaction is

Performance Outcomes and Measures

- We are the preferred supplier
- Customer satisfaction
- Internal customers use us
- Repeat business

8. Ensuring Compliance with the Law

Main Tasks

- Ensuring compliance with laws and regulations (e.g., EEOC, restraint of trade)
- Setting up systems and reporting mechanisms to ensure compliance
- Monitoring compliance performance
- Sustaining the ethics and values of the organization

Performance Outcomes and Measures

- Amount and cost of litigation
- Company's reputation in the business world

Core Competencies Identified as Most Important for Executive Team

1. Fostering Teamwork

Definition: As a team member, the ability and desire to work cooperatively with others on a team; as a team leader, demonstrating interest, skill, and success in getting groups to learn to work together cooperatively.

Behaviors for Team Members

- Listens and responds constructively to other team members' ideas.
- Offers support for others' ideas and proposals.
- Is open with other team members about his/her concerns.
- Expresses disagreement constructively (e.g., by emphasizing points of agreement, suggesting alternatives that may be acceptable to the group).
- Reinforces team members for their contributions.
- Gives honest and constructive feedback to other team members.
- Provides assistance to others when they need it.
- Works for solutions that all team members can support.
- Shares his/her expertise with others.
- Seeks opportunities to work on teams as a means to develop experience and knowledge.
- Provides assistance, information, or other support to others to build or maintain relationships with them.
- Is a source of ideas for accomplishing team goals.

Behaviors for Team Leaders

- Provides opportunities for people to learn to work together as a team.
- Enlists the active participation of everyone.
- Promotes cooperation with other work units.
- Ensures that all team members are treated fairly.
- Provides direction for the team and feedback on progress toward goals.
- Represents the team to management and is responsible for aligning the team goals to business objectives.
- Recognizes and encourages the behaviors that contribute to teamwork.
- Sponsors the development of teams.
- Pulls together a team comprised of the right combination of people to achieve a particular result.

2. Fostering New Ways (Combination of competencies #5 Managing Change and #24 Fostering Innovation)

Definition: Demonstrating support for innovation and for organizational changes needed to improve the organization's effectiveness; supporting, initiating, sponsoring, and implementing organizational change; helping others to successfully manage organizational change.

Employee Behaviors

- Personally develops a new method or approach.
- Proposes new approaches, methods, or technologies.
- Develops better, faster, or less expensive ways to do things.

Manager/Leader Behaviors

- Works cooperatively with others to produce innovative solutions.
- Takes the lead in setting new business directions, partnerships, policies, or procedures.
- Seizes opportunities to influence the future direction of an organizational unit or the overall business.
- Helps people to develop a clear understanding of what they will need to do differently, as a result of changes in the organization.
- Implements or supports various change management activities (e.g., communications, education, team development, coaching).
- Establishes structures and processes to plan and manage the orderly implementation of change.
- Helps individuals and groups manage the anxiety associated with significant change.
- Facilitates groups or teams through the problem solving and creative thinking processes leading to the development and implementation of new approaches, systems, structures, and methods.

3. Managing Performance

Definition: Taking responsibility for one's own or one's employees' performance, by setting clear goals and expectations, tracking progress against the goals, ensuring feedback, and addressing performance problems and issues promptly.

Behaviors for Employees

- With his/her manager, sets specific, measurable goals that are realistic but challenging, with dates for accomplishment.
- With his/her manager, clarifies expectations about what will be done and how.
- Enlists his/her manager's support in obtaining the information, resources, and training needed to accomplish his/her work effectively.
- Promptly notifies his/her manager of any problems that affect his/her ability to accomplish planned goals.
- Seeks performance feedback from his/her manager and from others with whom he/she interacts on the job.
- Prepares a personal development plan with specific goals and a timeline for their accomplishment.
- Takes significant action to develop skills needed for effectiveness in current or future job.

Behaviors for Managers:

- Ensures that employees have clear goals and responsibilities.
- Works with employees to set and communicate performance standards that are specific and measurable.
- Supports employees in their efforts to achieve job goals (e.g., by providing resources, removing obstacles, acting as a buffer).
- Keeps informed about employees' progress and performance through both formal methods (e.g., status reports) and informal methods (e.g., management by walking around).
- Provides specific performance feedback, both positive and corrective, as soon as possible after an event.
- Deals firmly and promptly with performance problems; lets people know what is expected of them and when.
- Fully implements the performance management goals in a timely way.
- Relates performance achievement to rewards and recognition.

4. Results Orientation

Definition: Focusing on the desired end result of one's own or one's unit's work; setting challenging goals, focusing effort on the goals, and meeting or exceeding them.

- Develops challenging but achievable goals.
- Develops clear goals for meetings and projects.
- Maintains commitment to goals, in the face of obstacles and frustrations.
- Finds or creates ways to measure performance against goals.
- Exerts unusual effort over time to achieve a goal or result.
- Has a strong sense of urgency about solving problems and getting work done.
- Consistently meets or exceeds the goals set.

5. Influencing Others

Definition: The ability to gain others' support for ideas, proposals, projects, and solutions.

- Presents arguments that address others' most important concerns and issues and looks for win-win solutions.
- Involves others in a process or decision to ensure their support.
- Offers trade-offs or exchanges to gain commitment.
- Identifies and proposes solutions that benefit all parties involved in a situation.
- Enlists experts or third parties to influence others.
- Develops other indirect strategies to influence others.
- Knows when to escalate critical issues to own or others' management, if own efforts to enlist support have not succeeded.
- Structures situations (e.g., the setting, persons present, sequence of events) to create a desired impact and to maximize the chances of a favorable outcome.
- Works to make a particular impression on others.

- Identifies and targets influence efforts at the real decision makers and those who can influence them.
- Seeks out and builds relationships with others who can provide information, intelligence, career support, potential business, and other forms of help.
- Takes a personal interest in others (e.g., by asking about their concerns, interests, family, friends, hobbies), to develop relationships.
- Accurately anticipates the implications of events or decisions for various stakeholders in the organization and plans strategy accordingly.

6. Establishing Focus

Definition: The ability to develop and communicate goals in support of the business's mission.

- Acts to align own unit's goals with the strategic direction of the business.
- Ensures that people in the unit understand how their work relates to the business's mission.
- Ensures that everyone understands and identifies with the unit's mission.
- Ensures that the unit develops goals and a plan to help fulfill the business' mission.

7. Decisiveness

Definition: Willingness to make difficult decisions in a timely manner.

- Is willing to make decisions in difficult or ambiguous situations, when time is critical.
- Takes charge of a group when it is necessary to facilitate change, overcome an impasse, face issues, or ensure that decisions are made.
- Makes tough decisions (e.g., closing a facility, reducing staff, accepting or rejecting a high-stakes deal).
- Consistently makes the best business decision in a timely manner.

8. Empowering Others

Definition: Conveying confidence in employees' ability to be successful, especially at challenging new tasks; delegating significant responsibility and authority; allowing employees freedom to decide how they will accomplish their goals and resolve issues.

- Gives people latitude to make decisions in their own sphere of work.
- Is able to let others make decisions and take charge.
- Encourages individuals and groups to set their own goals, consistent with business goals.
- Expresses confidence in the ability of others to be successful.
- Pushes decision making down to the lowest appropriate level.
- Encourages groups to resolve problems on their own; avoids prescribing a solution.
- Provides feedback on how the empowered individual is progressing.

9. Strategic Thinking

Definition: Analyzing our competitive position by considering the market and industry trends, our existing and potential customers, and our strengths and weaknesses as compared to competitors.

- Understands the organization's strengths and weaknesses as compared to competitors.
- Understands industry and market trends affecting the organization's competitiveness.
- Has an in-depth understanding of competitive products and services within the marketplace.
- Develops and proposes a long-term (3–5 year) strategy for the organization, based on an analysis of the industry and marketplace and the organization's current and potential capabilities as compared to competitors.

10. Entrepreneurial Orientation

Definition: A tendency to look for and seize profitable business opportunities; willingness to take calculated risks to achieve business goals.

- Notices and seizes profitable business opportunities.
- Keeps abreast of business, industry, and market information that may reveal business opportunities.
- Demonstrates willingness to take calculated risks to achieve business goals.
- Proposes innovative business deals to potential customers, suppliers, and business partners.
- Encourages and supports entrepreneurial behavior in others.

11. Persuasive Communication

Definition: The ability to plan and deliver oral and written communications that are impactful and persuasive with their intended audiences.

- Identifies and presents information or data that will have a strong effect on others.
- Selects language and examples tailored to the level and experience of the audience.
- Selects stories, analogies, or examples to illustrate a point.
- Creates graphics, overheads, or slides that display information clearly and with high impact.
- Presents several different arguments in support of a position.

12. Customer Orientation

Definition: Demonstrated concern for satisfying one's external and/or internal customers.

- Lives the business mission: to be the preferred supplier through total customer satisfaction.
- Quickly and effectively solves customer problems.
- Talks to customers (internal or external) to find out what they want and how satisfied they are with what they are getting.
- Shows flexibility in working with customers to meet their needs.
- Finds ways to measure and track customer satisfaction.
- Makes it easy for customers to do business with us.

13. Flexibility

Definition: Openness to different and new ways of doing things; willingness to modify one's preferred way of doing things.

- Is able to see the merits of perspectives other than his/her own.
- Demonstrates openness to new organizational structures, procedures, and technology.
- Switches to a different strategy when an initially selected one is unsuccessful.
- Demonstrates willingness to modify a strongly held position in the face of contrary evidence.

Team Competencies

To be an effective team member or team leader requires unique competencies that may differ from those required of an individual contributor or a manager. The following list is an example of team competencies from one organization. Note that some of the competencies combine several from our list of 31.

COACHING FOR TEAM EFFECTIVENESS

Team Member Competencies

1. Technical Expertise

Definition: Competencies that contribute to task accomplishment.

- Customer knowledge
- Technology
- Materials
- Quality theory and methods
- Business management

2. Initiative

- Identifies what needs to be done and does it; fills operational gaps.
- Challenges or changes internal processes that do not work.
- Shows a strong sense of urgency about getting the job done.
- Keeps focused on goals despite adversity.

3. Fostering New Ways (Combination of competencies #5 Managing Change and #24 Fostering Innovation)

- Tries new approaches that may enhance quality or efficiency.
- Makes and accepts suggestions for improvement/change and implements them if possible.

- Utilizes available technology to the fullest extent.
- Measures performance against a quantified standard and makes adjustments accordingly.

4. Customer Orientation

- Focuses efforts on meeting the needs of the customer.
- Emphasizes viewing problems from the standpoint of impact on the customer.
- Considers multiple business factors (e.g., long-term and short-term inputs; organizational consequences and financial consequences) when weighing alternatives.
- Translates technical and operational issues into business opportunities, risks and strategies.
- Views situations from the standpoint of their overall business impact.

5. Solving Problems Cluster

Definition: Diagnostic Information Gathering, Analytical Thinking, Conceptual Thinking.

- Evaluates and assimilates diverse sources of relevant information to develop an accurate understanding of issues and problems.
- Identifies the underlying causes of problems.
- Tackles a complex problem by breaking it into manageable parts.
- Carefully weighs the priority of things to be done.
- Discriminates between critical and non-critical issues.
- Anticipates the consequences and possible problems that may follow from taking a course of action.
- Steps back from the details of a problem and considers the larger picture of what is happening.

6. Flexibility

- Sees the merits of other, different perspectives.
- Shows openness to new organizational structures, procedures, and technology.
- Switches to a different strategy, if the current one is unsuccessful.
- Modifies a strongly held position in the face of contrary evidence.
- Revises existing plans and shifts priorities to meet new opportunities.
- Encourages diversity of thinking within the team.
- Identifies, respects, and utilizes interpersonal differences.

7. Fostering Teamwork

Definition: Effective interaction with others.

- Willingly provides assistance, knowledge, information, or support to other team members.
- Enlists active support and involvement of other team members.

- Clarifies own responsibilities and accountabilities to team.
- Reinforces teammates for their contributions and accomplishments.
- Listens attentively to all viewpoints, while withholding judgment..
- Communicates urgency and enthusiasm about the team's work.
- Supports a consensus decision, even if he/she personally disagrees with it.

8. Interpersonal Awareness

- Understands and addresses the most important concerns of others.
- Understands and responds to what others are feeling, based on their choice of words, tone of voice, and other nonverbal behavior.
- Listens actively, with full attention, attempting to see things from the speaker's point of view, and attending to the total communication, including body language and tone.
- Understands both the strengths and weaknesses of others.
- Talks to team members informally to learn how they are feeling.
- Anticipates how others will react to a situation.

9. Communications

Definition: Attention to Communication and Persuasive Communication.

- Conveys ideas in a clear, concise, honest, and relevant manner, orally and in writing.
- Asks questions to clarify expectations, rationales, and processes.
- Explains reasons for actions and decisions.
- Advocates effectively, by clearly explaining a position and its advantages as compared with alternatives.
- Communicates specialized technical knowledge by distilling essential points or concepts needed for understanding.
- Organizes and presents information in a way that enables the team to make a decision.
- Asks for, listens to, and utilizes feedback from others, regardless of level, without being defensive.
- Provides ongoing, positive, and constructive feedback.

10. Influencing Others

- Offers arguments that address others' most important concerns and issues.
- Looks for and proposes win-win solutions.
- Builds and maintains credibility by making commitments and delivering on them.
- Tailors words or actions to achieve a desired impact.
- Persuades by confidently presenting well-reasoned arguments.

Position Analysis

A key step in filling a position with someone who will meet your expectations is to accurately and thoroughly determine the requirements of the position. If you miss the mark here, there is a good chance that you will place an otherwise good candidate in the wrong position. In other words, you will not have a match.

The following analysis process is different from many others. It is designed to ensure that you will have the data you need to accurately analyze your open position.

It is organized into the following sections:

- The Company
- The Position
- Requirements
- Compensation
- The Location
- Search Strategy

1

THE COMPANY

HISTORY

_____
_____
_____
_____
_____
_____
_____
_____
_____

STRATEGY
Vision, Mission, Strategy, Goals

_____
_____
_____
_____
_____
_____
_____
_____
_____

BUSINESS REQUIREMENTS
Stakeholder Expectations

_____
_____
_____
_____
_____
_____
_____
_____
_____
_____

STRUCTURE
How is the company structured?

_____
_____
_____
_____
_____
_____
_____
_____
_____
_____

BUSINESS RESULTS

_____
_____
_____
_____
_____
_____
_____
_____
_____

CULTURE
How does the organization really operate?
What's it like to work here?

_____
_____
_____
_____
_____
_____
_____
_____
_____

2

THE POSITION

STRATEGY

How does this position impact the company's strategy? What is the department's strategy or how does this position impact it?

_____

_____

_____

_____

_____

_____

_____

_____

PURPOSE

Why does this position exist?

_____

_____

_____

_____

_____

_____

_____

_____

_____

OUTCOMES

At the end of the first year, what do you expect this person to have achieved? Number in priority order. Make as measurable as possible.

_____

_____

_____

_____

_____

_____

_____

_____

KEY SUCCESS FACTORS

What actions/behaviors/attitudes will contribute to success in this position?

_____

_____

_____

_____

_____

_____

_____

_____

_____

KEY "NO-NO'S"

What does the person in this position have to avoid doing in order to keep out of trouble?

_____

_____

_____

_____

_____

_____

_____

_____

_____

_____

_____

_____

_____

_____

_____

_____

_____

2
THE POSITION

REPORTING RELATIONSHIPS

3

REQUIREMENTS

COMPETENCIES

Competency Assessment

Consider all the attributes that are necessary for this position and rate each attribute on the following scale by circling the appropriate number.

1-2-3-4-5-6-7   Where 4 = Average importance to position
6 to 7 = Essential—can't be hired without these skills
1 to 2 = Not as important and/or are trainable

In addition, as you rate these attributes, indicate any that you feel are redundant by writing in the question number of the previous attribute that covers that topic.

To what extent is this competency required for performance as a _____

RATINGS	COMPETENCIES	COMMENTS Why is it important?
1 2 3 4 5 6 7	1. **Establishing Focus.** Developing and communicating goals in support of the business' mission	
1 2 3 4 5 6 7	2. **Providing Motivational Support.** Enhancing others' commitment to their work	
1 2 3 4 5 6 7	3. **Fostering Teamwork.** Getting groups to learn to work together cooperatively	
1 2 3 4 5 6 7	4. **Empowering Others.** Conveying confidence in employees' ability to be successful, allowing employees freedom to decide how they will accomplish their goals and resolve issues	
1 2 3 4 5 6 7	5. **Managing Change.** Initiating, sponsoring, or championing organizational change; helping others to successfully manage organizational change	
1 2 3 4 5 6 7	6. **Developing Others.** Delegating responsibility and coaching others to develop their capabilities	
1 2 3 4 5 6 7	7. **Managing Performance.** Providing employees with clarity about expectations and clear feedback about performance; dealing firmly and appropriately with performance problems	
1 2 3 4 5 6 7	8. **Attention to Communication.** Ensuring that information is passed on to others who should be kept informed	

RATINGS	COMPETENCIES	COMMENTS	Why is it important?
1 2 3 4 5 6 7	9. **Oral Communication.** Expressing oneself clearly in conversations and interactions with others		
1 2 3 4 5 6 7	10. **Written Communication.** Expressing oneself clearly in business writing		
1 2 3 4 5 6 7	11. **Persuasive Communication.** Planning and delivering oral and written communications that persuade intended audiences		
1 2 3 4 5 6 7	12. **Interpersonal Awareness.** Noticing, interpreting, and anticipating others' concerns and feelings, and communicating this awareness empathetically to others		
1 2 3 4 5 6 7	13. **Influencing Others.** Gaining others' support for ideas, proposals, projects, and solutions.		
1 2 3 4 5 6 7	14. **Building Collaborative Relationships.** Developing and maintaining partnerships with others		
1 2 3 4 5 6 7	15. **Customer Orientation.** Demonstrating concern for satisfying one's external and/or internal customers		
1 2 3 4 5 6 7	16. **Diagnostic Information Gathering.** Identifying the information needed to clarify a situation, seeking that information from appropriate sources, and using skillful questioning to draw out the information		
1 2 3 4 5 6 7	17. **Analytical Thinking.** Approaching a problem by using a logical, systematic, sequential approach		
1 2 3 4 5 6 7	18. **Forward Thinking.** Anticipating the implications and consequences of situations and taking appropriate action to be prepared for possible contingencies		
1 2 3 4 5 6 7	19. **Conceptual Thinking.** Finding effective solutions by taking a holistic, abstract, or theoretical perspective		
1 2 3 4 5 6 7	20. **Strategic Thinking.** Analyzing competitive position by considering the market and industry trends, existing and potential customers, and strengths and weaknesses as compared to competitors		
1 2 3 4 5 6 7	21. **Technical Expertise.** Depth of knowledge and skill in technical area		
1 2 3 4 5 6 7	22. **Initiative.** Identifying what needs to be done and doing it before being asked or before the situation requires it		
1 2 3 4 5 6 7	23. **Entrepreneurial Orientation.** Looking for and seizing profitable business opportunities; taking calculated risks to achieve business goals		
1 2 3 4 5 6 7	24. **Fostering Innovation.** Developing, sponsoring, or supporting the introduction of new and improved methods, products, procedures, or technologies		

RATINGS	COMPETENCIES	COMMENTS Why is it important?
1 2 3 4 5 6 7	25. **Results Orientation.** Focusing on the desired result of one's own or one's unit's work; setting challenging goals, focusing effort on the goals, and meeting or exceeding them	
1 2 3 4 5 6 7	26. **Thoroughness.** Ensuring that one's own and others' work and information are complete and accurate; careful preparation for meetings and presentations; following up with others to ensure that agreements and commitments have been fulfilled	
1 2 3 4 5 6 7	27. **Decisiveness.** Making difficult decisions in a timely manner	
1 2 3 4 5 6 7	28. **Self Confidence.** Faith in one's own ideas and ability to be successful; taking an independent position in the face of opposition	
1 2 3 4 5 6 7	29. **Stress Management.** Functioning effectively when under pressure and maintaining self control in the face of hostility or provocation	
1 2 3 4 5 6 7	30. **Personal Credibility.** Demonstrating concern that one be perceived as responsible reliable, and trustworthy.	
1 2 3 4 5 6 7	31. **Flexibility.** Openness to different and new ways of doing things; willingness to modify one's preferred way of doing things	

32. List the technical expertise and specialized knowledge required to perform in this role:

_____
_____
_____
_____
_____
_____
_____

33. List any additional competencies that are not included above:

_____
_____
_____
_____
_____
_____
_____

	Desired	Minimum Required
34. **Work** **Experience**		
35. **Industry** **Experience**		
36. **Education**		
37. **Knowledge**		
38. **Other** (anything you have not as yet commented on)		

Rated By: Date:

4
COMPENSATION

BASE SALARY AND REVIEW POLICY

_____
_____
_____
_____
_____
_____
_____

BONUS, INCENTIVE COMPENSATION

_____
_____
_____
_____
_____
_____
_____

PERKS

_____
_____
_____
_____
_____
_____

VACATION

_____
_____
_____
_____
_____
_____

BENEFITS

_____
_____
_____
_____
_____
_____
_____

RELOCATION ALLOWANCES

_____
_____
_____
_____
_____
_____
_____

SPOUSE JOB FINDING ASSISTANCE

_____
_____
_____
_____
_____
_____
_____
_____
_____
_____
_____

5
THE LOCATION

Quality of life, i.e., climate, schools, community activities, recreation, crime, cost of living.

_____
_____
_____
_____
_____
_____
_____
_____
_____
_____
_____
_____
_____
_____
_____
_____
_____
_____
_____
_____
_____
_____
_____
_____
_____
_____
_____
_____
_____
_____

6
SEARCH STRATEGY

SELECTION PROCESS
Who will interview and have input into the hiring decision? Assessments/tests? Group interviews? Do you ask interviewers to complete a feedback form? How skilled are your interviews?

_____
_____
_____
_____
_____
_____
_____

TARGET COMPANIES

_____
_____
_____
_____
_____
_____
_____
_____
_____
_____

ADMINISTRATIVE DETAILS
Who will be the primary contact for scheduling interviews, approving expenses, etc.?

_____
_____
_____
_____
_____
_____
_____
_____
_____

A Note for Human Resource Professionals: Applications of Competency Modeling

WHAT ARE COMPETENCIES?

Over the past 25 years, organizations have created thousands of competency models for various positions. In effect, each of these models is a "blueprint" for outstanding performance—both in thought and action—for a given job.

A competency is an underlying skill, personal characteristic, or motive—demonstrated by various observable behaviors—that contributes to outstanding performance in a job. Job competence assessment is a technique for systematically identifying the critcal charateristics that contribute to outstanding job peformance.

In simple jobs, performance depends primarily on mastering the job tasks, and most of the associated competencies are skills needed to perform the job tasks. But in more complex jobs, additional competencies are important, including many that are not skills directly used in performing job tasks.

To fully understand the capability that a person must bring to a job, you must distinguish between the various levels and types of competencies. These distinctions have implications for selection, assessment, and development systems and programs. They also affect how you measure or assess each type of competency.

Different types of competencies predict the ability to demonstrate different types of job behaviors. For example, a planning competency predicts specific actions such as setting goals, assessing risks, and developing a sequence of actions to reach a goal. An influence competency predicts specific actions such as having an impact on others, convincing others to perform certain activities, and inspiring others to work toward organizational objectives.

Competency Levels

Competencies exist at different levels of personality, which are illustrated in the figure below.

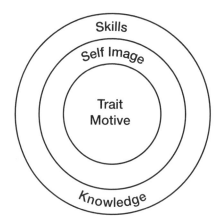

At the outer level are competencies that are defined in terms of skills or knowledge and are the easiest to develop. At an intermediate level are competencies defined in terms of self image, such as seeing oneself as a professional. Closer to the center are competencies defined in terms of personal traits such as taking initiative or demonstrating a concern for achievement or excellence. These competencies, personal traits, and motives are aspects of personality that are difficult to develop.

Examples of competency levels are as follows:

Behavioral

- Skills: An individual's ability to do something well.
  Example: Demonstrating a product.
- Knowledge: Information that an individual has in a particular area.
  Example: Having in-depth information about competitors.

Self-Concept: Attitudes and Values

- Self-Image: An individual's perception of his or her identity.
  Example: Seeing oneself as a "professional" (individual contributor) or a "manager."
- Occupational Preference: The work an individual values and enjoys.
  Example: Working with people instead of things.

Personal Characteristics

- Traits: A typical way of behaving.
  Example: Taking initiative.
- Motive: A fundamental and often unconscious "driver" of thoughts and behavior.
  Example: Concern for excellence.

Competency models identify competency types and levels for the job being assessed.

Motive and trait competencies are hard to develop; it is more cost-effective to select for these characteristics. Knowledge and skill competencies are relatively easy to develop; training is most cost-effective for these abilities. Self concept, attitude, and value competencies can be changed, although with more time and difficulty; these attributes are most cost effectively addressed by training with developmental job assignments.

Competencies that differentiate superior from average performance (differentiating competencies) and are hard to develop are most important for selection. Competencies more easily developed (minimal competencies) are less important for selection.

Minimal and differentiating competencies for a given job provide a template for personnel selection, succession planning, performance appraisal, and development.

Using the Competency Process to Drive Change

The process of identifying job requirements and required competencies means that the organization must first be clear about its short- and long-range direction. Once the direction is clear, it is important to determine the competencies that will be key to carrying out the organization's strategy and reaching its long-range goals. These competencies may differ from what had been important in the past. In fact, the process of developing competency models may indirectly force the organization to think through its strategy.

In order to carry out the strategy, it then becomes critical to build human resource support systems that enable the organization to:

- assess the competencies of current employees
- fill positions with people possessing the required competencies
- reward employees who meet job goals and develop competencies
- provide training and development experiences that build the key competencies.

CREATING AN INTEGRATED HUMAN RESOURCE SYSTEM

An integrated human resource system is a comprehensive set of human resource functions and programs that:

- share a common architecture or "language," and
- are organized to complement and reinforce one another.

This integration of HR information systems and programs contrasts with the typical system in which functions do not share a common language or complement one another; e.g., in which selection decisions are made on one set of criteria, performance is appraised on a second set of criteria, the training function teaches a third set of skills, etc. An integrated use of the competency assessment process is shown on the next page.

Integrated Uses Of Job Competency Assessment

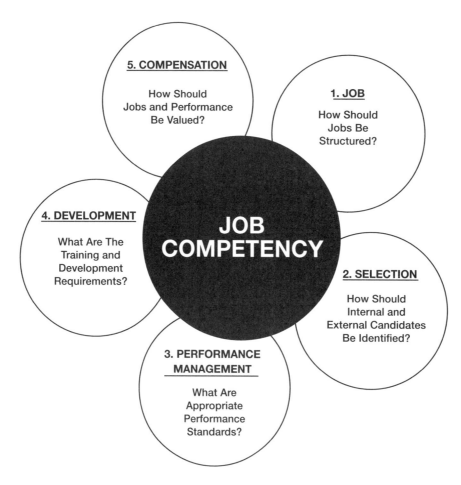

The "nucleus" of an integrated human resource system is a set of core data about job elements, including:

- Purpose
- Content—tasks, responsibilities, and functions
- Performance—standards and measures
- Measurement—points for compensation
- Competency requirements—the skills and characteristics that predict effective and superior performance in the job
- Employee competencies—the skills and characteristics individuals bring to their jobs

Job elements are determined by a firm's strategy and structure (design). Job element variables in turn drive the firm's human resource planning and human resource management functions such as recruitment, selection and placement, performance appraisal, development, succession planning, and support activities.

Development of an integrated human resource system usually begins with two initial steps:

1. ORGANIZATION STRATEGY—Selecting the criteria to define an organization's current success and its anticipated success over the next 5–10 years. This step includes plans for ways the firm will attain its goals. For example, a firm may project a significant amount of future growth dependent on the firm's ability to attract, develop, and retain good people in key positions.

2. ORGANIZATION AND JOB DESIGN—Defining ways the firm will organize itself to carry out its plans, with emphasis on identifying critical jobs such as the value-added "make or break" positions and people who will make the biggest difference in whether the firm succeeds or fails. Human resource management is most cost-effective when it focuses on these jobs.

Steps 1 and 2 are usually performed by reviewing a firm's business plans and interviewing its leadership.

Benefits of an Integrated Human Resource System

These benefits include:

- Cultural change and organizational improvement. Rather than being a barrier to change (as is the perception of human resource systems and functions in some organizations), a competency-based integrated human resource system provides a supportive link to the organization's strategic direction. Selecting and developing competent people produces a competent organization. A competent organization is more likely to survive in a highly competitive global economy.
- Cost savings/increased productivity. Separate functions do not develop and maintain duplicate (and often competing) databases, training, and administrative overhead.
- Empowered management. The tools and language of HR management are clearly defined and communicated; by understanding more of it, managers use more of it.
- Employee participation and reinforcement. Employees participate in the studies that define selection, compensation, appraisal, and development criteria; every employee contact with the HR system consistently communicates and reinforces these criteria.

HOW TO DEVELOP COMPETENCY MODELS

Competency models should focus on one critical job family, which should be identified by the company and is often used as a pilot program.

A job competence assessment usually includes some of the following steps:

1. DEFINE PERFORMANCE EFFECTIVENESS CRITERIA. To identify superior job incumbents, it is first necessary to define measures of performance effectiveness in a given job. The criteria typically include a combination of "hard" outcome measures such as sales or productivity data and nominations from management and peers.

2. IDENTIFY COMPARISON SAMPLES FOR INTERVIEWS. Job incumbents who are consistently rated superior on a number of different performance criteria provide a "template" standard for comparison analysis with a sample of average performers in the following steps of the research process.

Samples for job families should include superior and average performers at key ascension levels, e.g., from trainee to branch manager:

Level	Superior	Average
1. Trainee	8	5
2.	8	5
3.	8	5
4. Branch Manager	8	5
Totals	32	20

3. EXPERT PANELS. Managers and knowledgeable employees are asked to identify key aspects of each job, such as main responsibilities, most challenging situations, "feeder" jobs and the competency requirements (behaviors and characteristics) employees need to perform at an adequate or "threshold" level and at a superior level in the job.

Use of expert panels to define job elements offers a number of benefits. Panels collect much valuable data quickly and efficiently. Participation in panel sessions educates panel members in HR assessment methods and variables and, through involvement, develops consensus and support for overall project findings and recommendations.

4. COMPETENCY REQUIREMENTS SURVEY. A survey administered to all job incumbents and to their managers can be used to validate job elements identified by the expert panel. Surveys permit collection of sufficient data to do statistical analysis and have the added value of broad employee participation, which builds support for survey findings.

5. KEY EVENT INTERVIEWS. Superior performers and sometimes average performers in the designated job family are interviewed in a special type of interview designed to elicit detailed accounts of what employees did in successful projects and situations. The Key Event Interview asks interviewees to:

A. Identify the most critical situations they have encountered in their jobs and describe these situations in considerable narrative detail:

- What led up to the situation?
- Who was involved?
- What did the interviewee think about, feel, and want to accomplish in dealing with the situation?
- What did he or she actually do?
- What was his/her thought process at key points within the event?
- What was the outcome of the incident?

B. Identify the key developmental steps and experiences in their careers that led to their current job.

The Key Event Interview protocols also provide a wealth of data for the identification of competencies and very specific descriptions of critical job behaviors in specific situations. Interviewees' career paths can be analyzed to determine when, where, and how they acquired key competencies. A significant by-product of these interviews is the generation of numerous situation and problem narratives that can be used to develop highly relevant training materials, e. g., case studies, role plays, and simulations.

This interview method often identifies competencies that are different from those generated by panels. In addition, the interviews reveal the specific behavioral ways in which each competency is demonstrated.

6. THEMATIC ANALYSIS AND DEVELOPMENT OF A "COMPETENCY MODEL" FOR THE JOB. Typically, two or more analysts examine the data from expert panels, surveys and Key Event Interviews and identify candidate competencies and behaviors that are more frequently demonstrated by superior performers than by average performers.

The output of the job analysis step is a comprehensive job competency model, which includes:

- Purpose and content of the job: tasks, responsibilities and performance measures for the job rated as to level, frequency, and importance in a form which can be used to compare the job's content with other jobs.
- Competency requirements: the skills and characteristics required for adequate and superior performance in the job.
- Career paths for the job, with focus on when, where, and how key competencies for the jobs are developed.

Designing a Model Building Process Tailored to Your Organization's Needs

Where appropriate, other sources of data can be used to create a competency model. These include:

- Interviews with people in similar jobs in other companies.
- Interviews with subordinates, supervisors or customers of persons in the target job.
- Focus groups of job incumbents.
- Review of competency models of similar jobs in other organizations.
- Literature searches.

A model can often be built quickly and at low cost through interviews with superior performers and a panel session with managers and job incumbents.

Sometimes, as with re-engineering, new jobs are created for which there are few, if any, precedents. In such cases, it is useful to have a resource panel review a set of generic competencies, such as the 31 core competencies described in this book. It is also valuable to draw on the experience of consultants or other professionals with experience analyzing jobs in other organizations.

Application: Career Pathing and Succession Planning

The objective is to provide senior management with a system for providing and identifying a pool of ready replacements for key jobs, and to provide professionals with a clearly defined career path and a process to optimize their advancement. Key components may include:

- Detailed career paths with key job steps and profiles
- A process to identify ready replacements for next level jobs
- Development at rotational and temporary assignments, tasks, and training
- Communication packages for management and professionals
- Development of a 360° feedback tool based on the competency model
- A resource guide that participants and their managers can use to guide development planning
- Questions to guide participants through analysis of their assessment data and ultimately to a development plan
- Development planning forms
- A workshop on development planning, during which participants receive competency feedback and training on development planning

Application: Recruitment and Selection

Competency-based recruiting systems usually focus on screening methods used to winnow a small number of strong candidates from large numbers of applicants quickly and efficiently. Recruiting involves special challenges. For example, recruiters must screen many applicants within a short period of time. Also, applicants straight from college may have little work experience.

Competency-based recruiting systems, therefore, stress identification of competencies that meet the following criteria:

- Competencies that applicants will have had the opportunity to develop and demonstrate in their lives to date, whatever their jobs. Initiative is one example.
- Competencies that are likely to predict candidates' long-run career success and which are hard to develop through training or job experience. Concern for Excellence is an example.
- Competencies that can be reliably assessed using a short, targeted competency assessment interview developed for this purpose.

The competency assessment interview uses the same general approach as the Key Event Interview described earlier as a tool in building job models. The underlying assumption is that past performance is the best predictor of future performance. In a competency assessment interview, candidates are asked to describe their behavior in a particular type of situation. For example, the candidate might be asked to talk about a time he/she needed to convince someone to do something or about a time when he/she needed to solve a difficult problem. The types of situations asked about depend on the competencies being assessed.

The interviewer uses a probing strategy to obtain a detailed account of what the candidate did, said, and thought in the situation. To score the interview, the inerviewer compares the candidate's responses with specific categories of behavior that are criteria for the competency being assessed. For example, if the competency being assessed is Influence Skill, the criteria might include presenting compelling data and proposing solutions that address the other person's concerns.

Applications for the recruiting function can include:

- Integration of competencies into profiles developed by a recruitment and selection task force.
- Training for company recruiters to conduct and score competency assessment interviews to make screening decisions.
- Integration of applicant competency, tracking and administration information in the IHRS database, including follow-up evaluation of new hires to ensure recruiting system effectiveness.
- Tools to support an entire selection system, including formats to use in assessing screening candidates during interviews and in comparing and deciding among candidates.

Application: Performance Management

An additional human resource function that bears in important ways on development, retention, and career paths, is performance management. Competency assessment data can contribute to performance management systems in several ways, by identifying:

- Job performance standards and measures.
- Job behaviors required to accomplish specific job tasks and to meet job responsibilities.
- Competencies contributing to superior performance in key jobs.

Most performance appraisal systems assess one or more of these variables. Effective performance appraisal turns on the proper use of each type of data, given the objectives of the system and the degree of control the employee has over his or her performance on variables assessed.

Competency and job behavior data are usually used for decisions about development. For example, if a manager is appraised as lacking group leadership skills, he or she might be advised to attend a leadership course to develop this skill. Skill-based compensation systems also explicitly tie rewards to skills developed. This is particularly appropriate when employees have little control over performance results.

Applications planning for a company's performance management function can include:

- Identification of job responsibilities, performance standards and measures, and competencies to be appraised for employees in the target jobs.
- Development of appraisal methods and training of managers as needed. The entire process can be woven into a comprehensive performance management process (see p. 187).

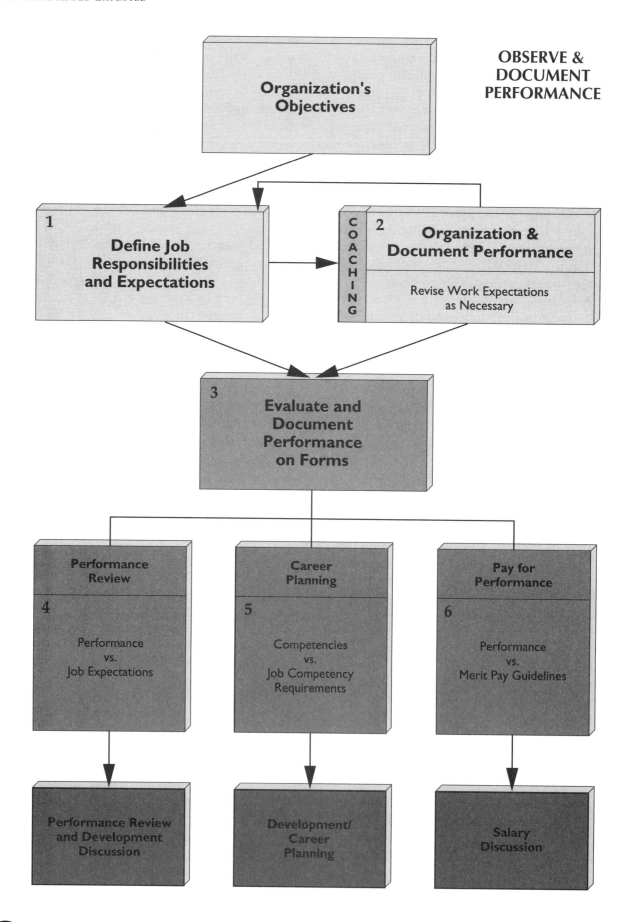

OBSERVE &
DOCUMENT
PERFORMANCE

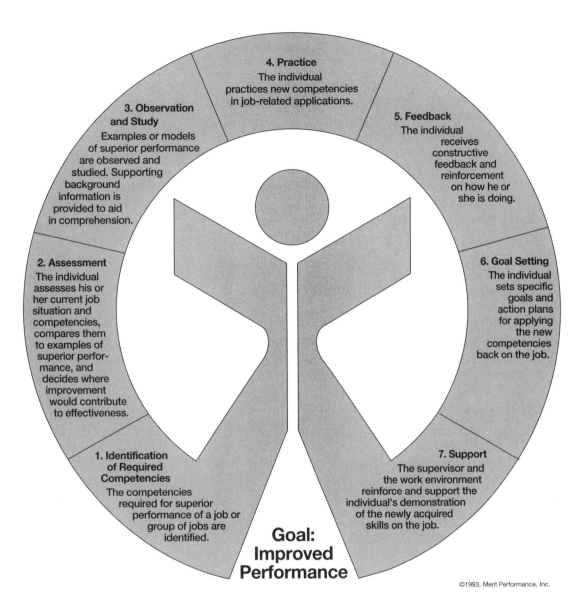

4. Practice
The individual practices new competencies in job-related applications.

3. Observation and Study
Examples or models of superior performance are observed and studied. Supporting background information is provided to aid in comprehension.

5. Feedback
The individual receives constructive feedback and reinforcement on how he or she is doing.

2. Assessment
The individual assesses his or her current job situation and competencies, compares them to examples of superior performance, and decides where improvement would contribute to effectiveness.

6. Goal Setting
The individual sets specific goals and action plans for applying the new competencies back on the job.

1. Identification of Required Competencies
The competencies required for superior performance of a job or group of jobs are identified.

7. Support
The supervisor and the work environment reinforce and support the individual's demonstration of the newly acquired skills on the job.

Goal: Improved Performance

©1993, Merit Performance, Inc.

A performance management program (for managers of persons in the target job) usually includes:

- Some training and/or exercises to familiarize managers with the competency model.
- Materials that clearly link the model to key job tasks and to performance standards.
- Training in a behavioral interviewing technique that the manager uses to get the direct report to talk in detail about how he/she approached key job tasks in specific instances.
- Training and practice for managers to help the direct report analyze his/her behavior on key job tasks and identify ways that the competencies were applied or could have been applied.

- A demonstration video showing how to conduct a performance management interview.
- Separate training on how to prepare for and hold a performance appraisal meeting.

Application: Training

The competency model becomes a framework for designing training activities. The competency modeling process provides a framework for a thorough analysis of training needs. A training needs analysis can then be used as a basis to develop a curriculum to help people acquire key competencies. A competency acquisition process for managing training efforts through increasing levels of competencies should consist of the seven steps outlined in the figure on the previous page.

SUMMARY

The output of a typical project might include:

- A comprehensive model of outstanding performance for a critical job family
- A Succession Planning and Career Pathing system
- System use of the model to enhance recruiting, selections, performance assessment, training, and development
- Transfer of technology to all staff
- Game plan for use of the process for other job families.

Index

About the Authors

Edward J. Cripe is president of Merit Performance, Inc., based in Fort Lauderdale, Florida. He has 30 years of experience in organization development, training, competency systems, performance management, and management consulting with companies such as ConAgra, American National Can, CIGNA, Ashland Oil, Cable and Wireless, and The Limited. He is the codeveloper of the REACH™ Coaching Performance Excellence training program and author of articles that have appeared in *Training and Development Journal, HR Professional, Corporate University Review,* and others.

Richard S. Mansfield, Ed.D., has more than 20 years of experience in competency-based job analysis, skills assessment, management development, and course development. He has completed major competency assessment and organizational change projects for clients in most industries, including American National Can, Digital Equipment Corp., EMC Corporation, The Travelers, Blue Cross-Blue Shield, and General Electric. Dr. Mansfield is co-author of *The Psychology of Creativity and Discovery* and has published numerous articles.